ASTROLOGY
FOR THE COSMIC SOUL

A Modern Guide to the Zodiac

THE PULP GIRLS

ROCK
POINT

Inspiring | Educating | Creating | Entertaining

Brimming with creative inspiration, how-to projects, and useful information to enrich your everyday life, quarto.com is a favorite destination for those pursuing their interests and passions.

First published in 2022 by Rock Point, an imprint of The Quarto Group,
142 West 36th Street, 4th Floor, New York, NY 10018, USA
T (212) 779-4972 F (212) 779-6058 www.Quarto.com

Rock Point titles are also available at discount for retail, wholesale, promotional, and bulk purchase. For details, contact the Special Sales Manager by email at specialsales@quarto.com or by mail at The Quarto Group, Attn: Special Sales Manager, 100 Cummings Center Suite 265D, Beverly, MA 01915 USA.

10 9 8 7 6 5 4 3 2 1

ISBN: 978-1-63106-885-0

Library of Congress Control Number:
2022935204

Publisher: Rage Kindelsperger
Creative Director: Laura Drew
Senior Managing Editor: Cara Donaldson
Editor: Keyla Pizarro-Hernández
Cover and Interior Design: Evelin Kasikov

Printed in China

This book provides general information on astrology. However, it should not be relied upon as recommending or promoting any specific diagnosis or method of treatment for a particular condition, and it is not intended as a substitute for medical advice or for direct diagnosis and treatment of a medical condition by a qualified physician. Readers who have questions about a particular condition, possible treatments for that condition, or possible reactions from the condition or its treatment should consult a physician or other qualified healthcare professional.

This is dedicated
to every Pulp babe that's
ever been and ever will be!
Thank you to all you cosmic hotties
from the bottom of our hearts
for being so damn supportive
and vibin' with our vibe.

Contents

Introduction

Hey there, cosmic hottie! We are so happy you're here, about to set off on a magical astrological journey with The Pulp Girls! So, who are we? We're Brianna and Cailie, the bestie-slash-sister duo behind the scenes here. The two of us have been working as a team to bring our creative visions to life since childhood. Starting at our creative roots writing, producing, and directing plays as kids, we've always been focused on making the world a bit more fun and a lot more self-confident! As teens, we began upcycling, styling, and selling vintage clothing. You could always find us with a camera in hand, drawing inspiration from vintage film and art. That dreamy, aesthetic world we were always seeking to create as kids? We found it within The Pulp Girls brand that grew out of our constant collaboration. There's something magical about finding a synergy with your bestie creative partner, a matching energy that constantly inspires and encourages the other person.

We've always found the idea of being able to fall into a different world within your own head impossibly fascinating. Transporting an audience to a perfectly aesthetic dream space is what we aim to do, whether that's a magical secret garden complete with fairies and frogs or a witchy 1970s arthouse film. Our goal with The Pulp Girls is to create the visual, visitable aesthetic world we ourselves have always dreamed of, and we're beyond elated to have other dreamers, like you, be a part of that special space!

So where does astrology come into all this, you might be asking? Well, did you read your horoscope when you were a kid? We definitely did! And checked out the bestie's sign, and maybe even looked at some compatibility with a crush. In the world of astrology, that's pretty basic stuff. Sure, we both knew our Sun signs. It was fun and we'd occasionally come across some weirdly accurate horoscope, but it didn't go much further than that until college, when we really began to get into astrology in depth. We were looking for a way to make observations about personality types and explore relationships and friendships. So we took the next natural step: we calculated our birth charts.

And, seeing that chart for the first time? It conjured up some serious math-class vibes, staring at some incredibly complex problem filled with lines, angles, symbols, and degrees.

Having only peeked at the occasional Sun sign horoscope in the past, we found trying to take in such an overwhelming amount of information, well, overwhelming! It's staggering to try to wrap your mind around it. And when you think about what that birth chart really is—you, in all your past, present, and future glory—it kinda makes sense that it's complicated. So, we kept at it. We kept learning and finding new inspiration in the world of astrology. It's a new way of understanding the wants and needs of people on a deeper level, and that's pretty dang awe-inspiring! The more we came to understand the foundations of astrology, the more we worked to meld that into our creations. For us, astrology and empowerment are a perfect union of self-reflection and discovery, something we lean into with everything we make.

No matter where you are in your astrological journey, we're here to deliver you some learning, some practical magic, and some straight-up zodiac fun! You hold in your hands your go-to guide for diving right on into astrology. Armed with this book, you'll be ready to strike up a conversation with just three little words: "What's your sign?"

Chapter 1

Astrology 101

Welcome to Astrology 101, where we'll be diving into the wonderful world of the zodiac! Astrology has been around for a while. Like, the hundreds-of-years-across-many-cultures kind of a while. Whether you believe the stars truly influence our lives or think of zodiac signs as more of a fun way to talk about people's personalities, you have to admit, astrology is here to stay. And why not? Astrology is just so dang fun! With people using astrology for everything from entertainment all the way on up to self-reflection, it's hard to deny the simple joy astrology brings to folks.

For many people, the zodiac experience begins with the Sun sign. This is the most common sign that horoscopes refer to, and it's definitely the easiest placement to figure out. All you need is a birth date and, voilà: Sun sign discovered, and the wide world of astrology memes unlocked. Getting into astrology gives you a whole new way to talk about yourself, your friends, and your relationships. Like, learning that your frenemy from middle school was a Libra. Or that your crystal-loving aunt is an Aquarius. It'll just make sense suddenly. Once you know, you just know. Soon, you'll be able to say, "Oh, you're *such* a Virgo!" to your bestie when she completely rearranges her closet yet again. You're equipping yourself with a totally new language for examining yourself and your relationships!

And we've got great news: Sun signs are just the tip of the astrological iceberg! There's a lot more to it than where the Sun was when you took your first breath.

After all, there are only twelve recognized signs and definitely more than twelve personalities out there. Calculating your birth chart reveals a great amount of information, especially when you first start learning about astrology. All the planets combine in vastly different ways for each person. Haven't you ever wondered why you click with one person so well, while another person drives you up a wall? Or why you beat yourself up over the smallest mistake? Why you need certain things to feel safe and secure, while your friends seem to need something very different? Learning about each zodiac sign allows you to understand how all your placements come together to make you uniquely you.

So, first things first! We've outlined a step-by-step recipe for you to get that all-important astrology tool: Your birth chart. Let's dive right in!

Getting That Birth Chart, Baby

Happy birthday cutie—belated, early, or otherwise! What day did you grace the planet with your presence? What time? Where? Not to get too invasive, but you need all this information to calculate your birth chart. Your birth chart is truly the key to unlocking all your astrological information. It's a picture of what was going on in the heavens at the exact moment of your first breath of life. (So yes, this includes natural births and C-sections and whatever else.) What were all the planets up to when your beautiful self finally got here? What kind of energy was flowing? If you've never generated your birth chart before, take a few minutes to do so right now. You're going to need your chart to really use this book. Find your birth certificate and follow this recipe to get that special map of you!

Birth Chart Recipe

Ingredients

Date of birth   Time of birth   Place of birth

Directions

1. Gather all your ingredients. Be as exact as possible!
2. Search the internet for a birth chart calculator. (It may also be referred to as a natal chart.)
3. Take screenshots of your whole chart. Yes, this is a LOT of information to take in! Don't stress; we're sticking to the basics.
4. That's it! We'll focus on what is generally known as the Big Three: your Sun sign, Moon sign, and Rising sign, also known as the Ascendant.

You should have a circle graph with a lot of lines and points. To find your Big Three, look for the following symbols:

Sun   Moon   Ascendant

Each of these symbols will fall within an astrology sign. Most online calculators will let you know where each sign falls, but it's always good to learn to read the chart. If you're looking for more help with the symbols, check the mini glossary at the back of this book (page 190).

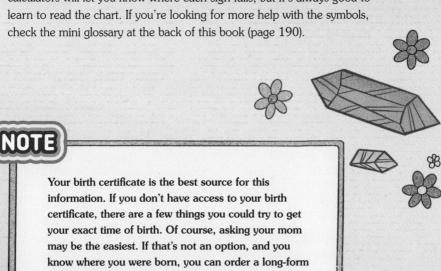

NOTE

Your birth certificate is the best source for this information. If you don't have access to your birth certificate, there are a few things you could try to get your exact time of birth. Of course, asking your mom may be the easiest. If that's not an option, and you know where you were born, you can order a long-form birth certificate and specifically request your birth time be included on it. If all else fails, you can look into birth time rectification, where an astrologer works backward through the events of your life to find your likely birth time.

The Language of Astrology

Okay, so now you've got a crazy, complicated-looking chart. How do you decipher all that? Let's all go back to the classroom really quick and do some Astrology 101. To get the most out of this book, you need to know just what we mean by your signs. As with any new language, learning about astrology can feel like a lot of information coming at you all at once.

There are all the zodiac signs, house systems, elements, modalities, aspects, cool symbols, and charts with lines all over them. Luckily, there's no reason whatsoever to cram all that information into your brain at once. Learning anything takes time, and astrology is no different. In fact, it's kind of something that only snaps into place as you grow and learn to understand yourself.

We're devoting entire sections to breaking down the Sun, Moon, and Rising signs, so you can read about your personal planets in depth. These three placements, along with your Mercury, Venus, and Mars placements, have the most direct influence on your life. When you're just starting out on your astrological journey, it's best to focus on exploring the Big Three placements. Before we get there, however, let's take a quick dive into modalities and elements, two concepts that lend each individual sign its own flavor and way of influencing the world, as well as the vibes of each planet.

Modalities

There are three types of modalities in astrology: cardinal, fixed, and mutable. The best way to think about modality is in terms of the seasons. Cardinal signs always kick off the season, so they express their energy by starting things, by initiation. Fixed signs hold things nice and steady, right in the middle of the season. And mutable signs oversee the shift from one season to the next. They lean into that adaptability, embracing change and preparing for something new.

Cardinal signs are the initiators of the zodiac. Essentially, all cardinal signs are driven to *do*, to use the energy at their disposal.

- **Aries**, the first sign of spring, is all about hitting the ground running as things spring to life.
- **Cancer** kicks off summer, with its ability to reach out and make emotional connections.
- **Libra** ushers in autumn, aka cuffing season: developing relationships is Libra's forte.
- **Capricorn** brings winter and is famous for its ability to initiate (and follow through on) long-term plans!

Fixed signs are situated right in the center of each season. They're solid, sustained, and dependable.

- **Taurus** is the embodiment of spring, employing the senses to shore up the beauty of the world.
- **Leo**, the quintessential summer sign, uses its exuberance and persona to keep the party going.
- Autumnal **Scorpios** stabilize the world via their own emotional acuity, never flinching from the darker side of things.
- **Aquarius** employs the cool power of its intellect to keep things running smoothly all winter.

Mutable signs exist in shifting times, as the seasons change. These guys excel at adapting, accepting change, and moving forward.

- Mercurial **Gemini** sees spring maturing to summer and loves to share all kinds of information.
- **Virgo** presides over the summer-to-autumn change, with a focus on sharing practical skills.
- **Sagittarius** is situated at the end of autumn, fostering cooperation and enthusiasm for the last days of harvest.
- **Pisces**, the dreamiest of signs, falls in that wistful period when winter begins to thaw into spring and all things start to seem possible.

Elements

The elements are the natural powers of the world that give each sign its unique flavor. There are four kinds of elements in astrology: fire, earth, air, and water. Fire signs burn bright, with a focus on self-expression and enthusiasm. Earth signs are the stabilizers of the zodiac, preferring practical, grounded things. Air signs are all about communication and intellect. Water signs process the world via emotion and intuition. When you combine your sign's modality and element, you get that gorgeous blend that makes you, you!

Fire
Aries, Leo, Sagittarius

As fire signs, these three zodiac placements share a love of spontaneity and expressiveness. They're all about warmth, illumination, and sometimes, being just a bit extra. Fire signs live life loudly and at high speed! They're known for being pretty courageous, self-sufficient, and maybe even a bit forceful. Aries is the cardinal fire sign, Leo is the fixed fire sign, and Sagittarius is the mutable fire sign.

Earth
Taurus, Virgo, Capricorn

Earth signs love some good, solid ground under their feet. They like practical things and real, measurable results. With a worldly concern for material things, earth signs know what they like and work hard to earn it. Creating order out of chaos gives these signs a sense of fulfillment. Taurus is he fixed earth sign, Virgo is the mutable earth sign, and Capricorn is the cardinal earth sign.

Air
Gemini, Libra, Aquarius

All kinds of information and communication fly through the airwaves, and air signs love it all. Each sign here is blessed with the gift of gab and an impressive intellect. They're charming and love nothing more than to get all the facts, reason things out, and see every side of life. Gemini is the mutable air sign, Libra is the cardinal air sign, and Aquarius is the fixed air sign.

Water
Cancer, Scorpio, Pisces

Swimming in the waters of emotion, these signs are naturally intuitive and ultra-empathetic. They prefer to act based on vibes, trusting in their gut feelings to give them an accurate reading of the situation. Whether they admit it or not, these signs tend to be very sensitive, which can manifest in mood swings or brooding silences. Cancer is the cardinal water sign, Scorpio is the fixed water sign, and Pisces is the mutable water sign.

The Planets and Their Vibes

In astrology, we're working with a lot of things, as you've probably noticed just by looking over your birth chart. At the core of everything astrology are the planets. These celestial bodies form the foundation for pretty much everything zodiac related. Each planet in our solar system, including the two luminaries (the Sun and the Moon), exerts its own particular influence on everything from your birth chart to your daily life. Understanding the basic vibe of each component in the sky is absolutely essential in your astrology journey. After all, each sign is ruled by one (or more) of these cosmic forces, and they all have their own "personalities," strengths, and weaknesses.

Sun

Influence: The "planet" of the self: personality and ego
Vibes: Illuminating and expressive
Rules: Majestic Leo

Moon

Influence: The "planet" of emotions: inner self and soul
Vibes: Reflective and nurturing
Rules: Intuitive Cancer

Mercury

Influence: The planet of communication: intellect and motion
Vibes: Restless and curious
Rules: Quick-witted Gemini and perceptive Virgo

Venus

Influence: The planet of love and money: romance and pleasure
Vibes: Refined and sensual
Rules: Exquisite Taurus and harmonious Libra

Mars

Influence: The planet of passion: action and drive
Vibes: Determined and ambitious
Rules: Fiery Aries and passionate Scorpio

Jupiter

Influence: The planet of luck: fortune and ideology
Vibes: Knowledgeable and benevolent
Rules: Charismatic Sagittarius and spiritual Pisces

Saturn

Influence: The planet of karma: discipline and responsibility
Vibes: Restrained and authoritative
Rules: Taskmaster Capricorn and responsible Aquarius

Uranus

Influence: The planet of rebellion: freedom and innovation
Vibes: Unconventional and trailblazing
Rules: Eccentric Aquarius

Neptune

Influence: The planet of illusion and escape
Vibes: Abstract and captivating
Rules: Dreamy Pisces

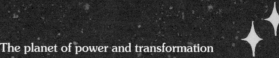

Pluto

Influence: The planet of power and transformation
Vibes: Destructive and regenerative
Rules: Transcendent Scorpio

Your Big Three: Sun, Moon, and Rising

Before we get into each individual sign, let's break down just what we mean when we're talking about Sun, Moon, and Rising signs. As we've mentioned, these are what we sometimes refer to as your "Big Three." These are the placements that have the greatest influence on your own day-to-day life because they inform so much of how you act and react. They fall under the umbrella of "personal planets," as opposed to "generational planets."

Okay, let's do some visualizing. You've seen a model of the solar system, right? The Sun is right in the middle, with everything else rotating around that central point. We start with Mercury, the closest planet to the Sun, and move further out into space, all the way out to cold, lonely Pluto. And that's not even touching on the various asteroids that make their way into astrology! For simplicity's sake, we'll stick to planets.

Obviously, since some planets are closer to the Sun than others, they make their way across our skies here on Earth more quickly than those outer planets do. These are your Sun, Moon, and Rising signs, as well as your Mercury, Venus, and Mars signs. In a birth chart, these placements can change very quickly, especially the Ascendant, or Rising sign. The travel time of the various planets is why your birth time is so essential for an accurate natal chart. The rest of the planets are "generational." Jupiter, Saturn, Uranus, Neptune, and Pluto all take much longer to traverse our skies. Jupiter shifts signs once every twelve years or so, while

Pluto, with its weird orbit, can linger in a placement for decades! These outer planets affect whole generations and are less personalized.

In this book, we will focus on your Sun, your Moon, and your Rising signs. Your Sun is the central self, your core identity. Just as that bright, beautiful Sun is the central point of our solar system, your Sun sign is the anchoring point around which all your other placements revolve. Everything in your chart wraps around that bright, glowing Sun sign. When you check your Sun in an astrology setting, you're looking at the ways you express your individuality, what makes you feel confident, and your self-image. This is an outward-facing placement, something that others see. The Sun has sway over your actions.

Your Moon, on the other hand, is your inner self, your emotional identity. The more self-awareness you practice, the more you'll feel connected to your Moon sign. This is a more private, intimate side of your personality. Other people tend to see this only when they are very close to you. Your Moon placement influences your reactions. How you process your feelings and relate to people on an instinctual level are due in large part to your Moon sign. Here, you tend to find insight into the kinds of structures, people, and patterns that allow you to feel a sense of stability in life. This is also a big one for relationship compatibility. When you're trying to figure out how to make someone feel seen and appreciated, check their Moon sign!

The final ingredient in your Big Three is your Rising sign. This placement is also sometimes called the Ascendant because this sign was literally ascending over the eastern horizon when you took your first breath. Your Rising sign is the mask you wear out in the world. These are the traits others see in you, so it has a big influence on things like physical appearance, mannerisms, and first impressions. When you see someone and think, oh, they *must* be a Pisces, only to find out they're a Libra Sun or another Sun sign, you might be picking up on their Rising sign. Your Rising is your vibe, your presence. It introduces you before you even speak.

Check the below cheat sheet when you're confused about what each of the Big Three influences.

Big Three Cheat Sheet

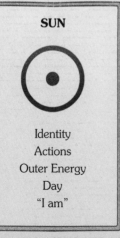

SUN

Identity
Actions
Outer Energy
Day
"I am"

MOON

Emotions
Reactions
Internal Dialogue
Night
"I feel"

RISING

Aura
Interactions
External Vibe
Dawn
"I act"

Sun Signs

Okay, now that you are equipped with enough astrology basics, let's get into Sun signs! Also sometimes referred to as your "star sign," or even simply "your sign," this is the placement used for the most popular form of astrology. It's by far the easiest one to figure out, as you can usually identify someone's Sun sign with just their birth date. And while it can be a tad generalized, many, many people of the same Sun sign tend to share certain traits.

Need a quick refresher? That's okay! Your Sun sign represents your core self. Like the Sun itself, this placement is at the heart of who you are. Your Sun sign informs your self-image, your confidence, and your overall direction in life. Pretty important stuff! Of course, people are far more complex than one zodiac sign. That's where your chart as a whole comes in. All your other planets orbit the Sun, adding their own flavor to the beautiful blend that makes you, you.

Still, you should always begin your astrological journey at the center: your Sun sign. It is absolutely essential to understanding your personality, after all. Everything else in your chart supports and influences this core self. We included the usual date ranges for each Sun sign, but the start and end date can shift a day or so depending on the year. So make sure you've calculated your birth chart, then flip to your Sun sign and get all the juicy details!

Sun in Aries

Aries is a cardinal sign ruled by the planet Mars. Remember your Greek mythology? Mars is the god of war, powered by action, competition, and taking initiative. You tend to be energetic and active. As a cardinal sign, you're driven to jump into new projects headfirst. Independence is probably up at the top of the list of things you can't live without, followed by a need to be around people who appreciate your enthusiasm. You're blessed with unquenchable *joie de vivre*, which can come across as an endearingly childlike eagerness for life . . . or as being totally extra.

Carrying all that spontaneous Mars energy means Aries tend to leap before they look. You've likely found yourself in over your head after some impulsive decisions! Luckily, you usually have a knack for getting yourself clear of any serious trouble. Aries are confident and brave, and their natural kinetic abilities make them resilient. Body-oriented Aries have a desire to do things physically, whether that's traditional athletics, dancing around wildly, or even using their hands to create!

Be careful of being a bit too "I'm always right." Aries sometimes seem like they were born conflict-ready. While you may enjoy making everything into a good, healthy competition, other folks can see you as aggressive, pushy, and overly combative. Learn to read the room! You're quite the courageous cutie, but it's important to remember that you are still human. You still need to take time for self-reflection, to process the things happening in your life.

Sun in Taurus

April 20–May 20
The Bull

You'd be hard-pressed to find someone more chill than a Taurus! This fixed earth sign is ruled by beauty-loving Venus. Sensual and imaginative, you understand that life is meant to be lived to the fullest. Taureans explore the world with all five senses, which means they tend to place a lot of importance on the material world and aesthetics. That impeccable taste extends to everything: Taurus always knows the best places to eat, makes the best playlists, and has the most luxurious recommendations. All Taureans have a secret (or not-so-secret) hedonistic streak. After all, life is beautiful and tantalizing; shouldn't it be enjoyed?

All earth signs are known for their reliability, and Taurus is no exception. You're incredibly trustworthy and you try your hardest to always follow through on what you promise. The need to stabilize, to create order out of the chaos, permeates a Taurus's life. Sudden changes and big risks upset that deep-seated need for stability and security. Beware the horns when you cross a Taurus. They don't like to be rushed! Nature takes its time and still gets everything done, after all. While Taurus gets the stereotype of being lazy, it's simply not true. Yes, you prefer to do things in your own time, but you're also willing to put in the work. You just like to work smarter, not harder.

Your perfect day would involve spending all day lounging somewhere serene and beautiful, surrounded by good friends, great food, and expensive wine. Nothing wrong with that! Taurus is willing to work hard to reap the rewards. As a fixed sign, you have a seriously legendary sense of determination and a willingness to do what needs to be done. From an outside perspective, however, it can be hard to differentiate between that willpower and stubbornness. It's difficult to budge a Taurus once they've made up their mind. Taureans tend to dig in their heels and simply refuse to entertain other ideas. The celestial bulls also have a reputation for possessiveness and jealousy. This most often stems from the desire for stability in life. It's important for Taureans to remember that change can be both good and necessary, and that there is enough for everyone.

Sun in Gemini

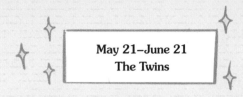

Gemini presides over the shift from spring to summer. Think about the vibe of that time of year: the days are longer, things are in bloom, school's getting out, summer plans are being made. The air is simply brimming with a sense of excitement and anticipation! As a Gemini, you're the most mercurial of all the signs. Ruled by Mercury, the god of communication and travel, Gemini approaches life with voracious curiosity and a deep desire for knowledge. You have a huge variety of interests and somehow end up being really good at practically anything you set your mind to. As a mutable sign, you're blessed with the gift of adaptability. You instinctively understand that growth is all about change, so you're able to roll with it when life throws you a curveball.

Mirroring their celestial counterpart, the twins, Geminis can have a dual nature. You might show one face to your family and become an entirely different person in social circles. This shape-shifting nature can make others uncomfortable, but it can also be a major asset. After all, being able to approach things from different viewpoints allows you to find solutions others might have missed. It also makes you pretty amazing at parties! You can read the vibe of the room with ease and slip into whatever role best fits the moment. Geminis have the gift of gab, whether you use it or not. With your innate desire to gather and share information, you always have a great story to tell, and maybe even some hot gossip. Be careful of going too far; it's important to temper your words with a bit of discretion sometimes.

You might feel like a walking contradiction at times, but that's really just your natural flexibility. You're somehow able to be both introverted and extroverted, serious and silly, and to see both sides of an argument and run with either. There's just so much out there in the world and Geminis want to experience it all! Geminis excel at out-of-the-box creative thinking. You have no problem starting all kinds of projects . . . but finishing them is another story. "Routine" might as well be a four-letter word as far as you're concerned, which can be frustrating for other people in your orbit. When you get too flighty or cerebral, remember to ground yourself, to check back in with your innermost needs and desires.

Sun in Cancer

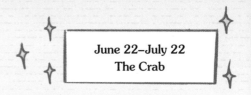

June 22–July 22
The Crab

As the cardinal water sign, Cancer places a high value on emotional bonds. By nature, you're a deeply nurturing person, with an instinctive understanding of what others need. It's uncanny how often you've picked up on a loved one's problems before they even realize something is wrong. Cardinal signs are all about initiation, and remember, you were practically born understanding the human need to create connections. Cancer is associated with the traditional role of the mother, which makes sense. You remember the little things that mean a lot, like birthdays, favorite foods, and that time you had a whole conversation via eye contact like five years ago. You also deal with the messy parts of human nature that others hide from. While other signs may have trouble with intense emotions, you confront them with staunch bravery. Life isn't always pretty, but you're going to be there for your loved ones regardless.

Cancers are known for their ability to create a warm, comforting sense of home. You understand the sense of community and love that comes from nourishing others, so even if you don't cook often, you're likely pretty good at it. Your home is your sanctuary, and you have trouble when things seem off or tense in your castle. You're the kind of person to have dream home mood boards and a secret love for all things romantic. You're a sucker for dramatic ride-or-die gestures, as you need reassurance that all that care you invest in others is given back to you in return.

Your sense of empathy is your power, but it can also be a curse without some solid boundaries. All that emotional heavy lifting can drag you down. Cancers have a reputation for moodiness, which comes from the tidal waves of emotions you take on to protect others. Giving so much of yourself inevitably comes with a lot of emotional exhaustion and melancholy. When you vent your frustrations, you tend to do it in an indirect way. After all, you work hard to avoid conflict, to keep everyone happy. Cancers would do well to remember that sometimes you will have to directly confront a situation, especially if you're running yourself ragged. Don't lash out with passive-aggressive attacks. Don't retreat into your shell. Use those strong connections you've made while still prioritizing your own needs.

Sun in Leo

Leo loves all things glamorous, regal, and dramatic. With your Sun in the sign of the lion, you shine brightly. There's no hiding the passion and power that run through your veins. Leos have an innate understanding of how they're perceived. Ever the showmen, Leos are natural performers. You understand that heads will turn toward the brightest light in the room, and that just so happens to be you! You have a flair for drama, for better or worse. As a fixed fire sign, you have a magical kind of staying power, which you use to become the best in whatever form of self-expression calls to you. Many Leos gravitate toward the spotlight, but really, you probably excel in everything you do. It's just part of that certain *je ne sais quoi* that makes you burn so brightly!

Leos are all about life, always bigger and better. You thrive on big plans, juicy drama, and treating yourself. When you surround yourself with people who reflect your inner beauty back at you, life feels truly amazing. When you allow other people to take your energy and never contribute anything in return, you become bitter and self-righteous. As a Leo, you're a natural mover and shaker, so you have the power to change your narrative. Cut out toxic folks and use your charisma to attract only people who help you shine.

This Sun placement loves to lavish their friends and loved ones with attention, gifts, and good times. And they expect it to be reciprocal: rightly proud of their abilities, Leos need to be appreciated for all they do. After all, giving so much of your light to the world deserves a round of applause! You're always open to a compliment because what's wrong with being admired? Leos have a deep-seated need for recognition, and when denied that, they can become somewhat egomaniacal and self-obsessed. While praises are always accepted, constructive criticism, even when it's well intentioned, can be taken as a personal attack. You're more sensitive than you allow the world to see, so it's important to remember that most people, especially those closest to you, are looking out for your best interests. Check yourself. Hear them out before you go off!

Sun in Virgo

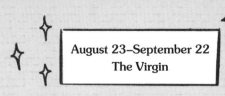

August 23–September 22
The Virgin

With your Sun in Virgo, you're blessed with both a selfless nature and a desire to make the world a better, more ordered place. You likely have extremely high standards, which more often than not go double for yourself. Virgos are famous perfectionists. You can't stand the idea of settling for "okay." Good luck finding anyone more dedicated and hardworking than a Virgo! You have an innate need to sort the disarray of life into neat, practical piles. It's all about refinement for you, because you know things could be better if people just tried. Your self-sacrificing nature manifests in just how much *you* try, despite knowing people will make mistakes and even the best-laid plans can go awry.

Virgo is ruled by Mercury, so while you're always brimming with ideas and a huge variety of skills, you're also prone to overthinking just about everything. Thoughts come fast and you're constantly processing information. Here's where the Virgo stereotype for being a neat freak comes in. You use the everyday routines of tidying and cleaning to scratch that itch for order in the chaos. Being able to see tangible, measurable results of your efforts is a big deal for you. You're an earth sign, after all, so you like things to be clear, grounded, and practical. People probably come to you for your amazing, well-thought-out advice. They know they can trust you to be helpful and supportive no matter what.

With all that mental energy swirling around, urging you to make things perfect, you need to put that energy into something that matters to you. Without a specific goal, you can fall prey to your own self-criticisms, spiraling down a rabbit hole of all your perceived flaws. This can also be turned outward when stressed, as you subject anyone around you to micromanagement and unsolicited criticism veiled as advice. Learn to forgive yourself and others. There's absolutely nothing wrong with being meticulous when you apply it in a healthy way! You have an unparalleled ability to solve problems and heal broken things.

Sun in Libra

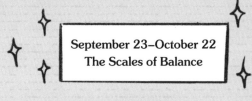

Ruled by Venus, the planet of love and beauty, Libra is all about symmetry and balance. Their astrological symbol is the scales, and nothing pleases them more than bringing everything around them into harmony. You're at your peak surrounded by beautiful things, intelligent people, and a high-class environment. And oh my gosh, do people like you! It seems so effortless, so natural! But the secret is, you actually do try pretty hard. You worry a lot about what other people think of you. You're kind of an expert at being what other people want you to be. However, you're still a human being with your own needs. Don't forget to speak up for yourself!

With your Sun in Libra, you're horrified by injustice of any kind. Your symbol is the scales, after all: you place a high premium on fairness and integrity. This works incredibly well with your natural objective nature. You can see all sides and don't mind sacrificing if it keeps the peace. Be careful of being *too* diplomatic, though; people won't trust you if they realize you've evaded an issue or omitted certain things, even if it was done for the sake of sparing feelings.

As a cardinal sign, Libra is big on relationships of all kinds. You're highly attuned to how others feel, so when things feel off, you jump right in to try to fix any and all problems. You're usually the mediator between bickering friends, using your natural charm to smooth out the kinks and create a pleasant atmosphere for everyone. This gift comes at a price, however: you work so hard to please others that your own needs are often neglected. You may also feel paralyzed by even the smallest decisions as you weigh everyone else's feelings and desires. It's admirable to try to avoid hurt feelings, but sometimes you need to just lay it out there. Disagreements and conflicts are part of life.

Sun in Scorpio

You've heard the phrase "still waters run deep," right? That's a Scorpio Sun in a nutshell. This fixed water sign is the epitome of deep and mysterious. Scorpios are famously alluring, beguiling, and magnetic, usually without even saying a word. This Sun placement values honesty above everything, with a deep need to learn exactly what makes other people tick. You love uncovering secrets and hidden motivations. You somehow intuit what others will say or do, so much so that you might have even felt you were psychic at times. That instinctive understanding of human nature is a water sign thing, but Scorpio combines that impressive empathy with some serious strategy. Your astrological symbol is the scorpion, and like the scorpion, you study how your target acts, conserving your power until just the right moment. You usually get what you want.

Scorpio is ruled by both Mars and Pluto. That fiery Mars energy manifests in your unmatched reserve of passion. Words like *intense* and *obsessive* are usually thrown around when talking Scorpio stereotypes. The truth is no one loves quite like a Scorpio! Absolutely devoted, once you're in, you're in for good. On the flip side, anyone who crosses a Scorpio better be ready to get stung. Scorpio never forgets anything and your ability to play the long game means you might be tempted to seek revenge. When underdeveloped, Scorpios can be very possessive, jealous, and ruthless. Be careful how you use your powers: getting even isn't the same as moving on or growing as a person.

Luckily, Pluto, the planet of death, rebirth, and transformation, lends Scorpio an incredible sense of resilience. You don't shy away from the darker side of humanity. You have an unbelievable capacity for taking trauma and pain, facing down fear and emotional intensity, and transforming all that into strength and healing. Like a phoenix rising from the ashes, you're able to embrace chaos and destruction and transmute it into something new and powerful. It's the secret behind your magnetism!

Sun in Sagittarius

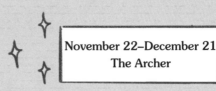

Sagittarius, the mutable fire sign, is symbolized by a centaur wielding a bow and arrow. You're always seeking something: adventure, knowledge, enlightenment, new horizons, or even just a good time! Willing to try anything once, you pursue variety in all aspects of life. This has earned Sagittarius its reputation for being hard to pin down, particularly in the realm of relationships. For the record, it's a total cliché that a Sagittarius runs away from any and all commitment. Sure, you don't want to be tied down. That's totally different from surrounding yourself with people who respect your need for independence while still keeping things fun! Sagittarius will stick around for the *right* people.

Given the freedom you require, you approach life from a place of optimism. Of course, everyone experiences struggles and unhappiness, but you don't like to wallow in those feels. You believe there's always something new around the corner, and you don't waste time getting to that new, better future. You're blessed with a serious wanderlust, which can manifest in actual travel, but also includes mental and spiritual journeys. Even if you don't care for the formal structure of school, you love acquiring knowledge.

Your natural wit and storytelling skills make you a born comedian. You've got a knack for lightening the atmosphere almost anywhere, and you attract friends with ease. You always have something to say, as you seem to know things about just about everything under the Sun. Unfortunately, your way with words can get you into trouble sometimes; Sagittarius does not sugarcoat the truth. You hate lying, even by omission. But honesty can be brutal, especially when someone can't handle it. Obviously, being truthful is always better than lying, but you need to learn to add a little bit of tact in with the facts. It's possible you don't know everything, as shocking as that sounds! Your good intentions can't make up for hurt feelings.

CAPRICORN

Sun in Capricorn

**December 22–January 19
The Sea Goat**

Overachieving Capricorns are talented at pretty much *everything* they set their minds to. You thrive when you focus on real, practical applications of your skills. Essentially, you feel fulfilled when you have a goal in sight and you're putting in the work. Of course, you like to see the results of all that hard work, but you can also play the long game. Good things take time, and you use your energy wisely. Capricorn is the mythological sea goat, meaning you're not scared of scaling lofty heights, nor do you shy away from creative potential. As a cardinal earth sign, you're out there setting long-term plans into motion, creatively employing whatever tools are available to you. It's no surprise that a great many successful people are Capricorns!

Self-restraint is huge for Capricorns. Emotions are usually kept on lock, especially when you're around people you don't know well. It's hard for you to devote your precious time and energy to things that don't work toward your life goals. While other placements may struggle to even establish boundaries, you are all about them. This is why you sometimes come across as ultra-serious or cold when others meet you. The truth is, it simply takes time for you to open up. After all, you need to make sure they're worth it! Once you let folks in, your quick mind and sharp wit make you the funniest low-key person in the room.

Capricorns are natural leaders, excellent at organizing everything from major projects to a game night with friends. You understand what it takes to get things done, and you're great at directing others. High expectations are a good thing, especially when it helps you reach your goals! However, underdeveloped Capricorns can fall prey to a "my way or the highway" mind-set. Your personal workaholic tendencies don't mean you can impose harsh, unrealistic standards on others. You can be prone to sullenness and brooding, especially if you feel like those standards aren't being met. If you always have your eyes on some distant prize, you can miss out on the good things surrounding you in the moment.

Sun in Aquarius

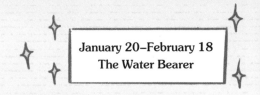

January 20–February 18
The Water Bearer

As the resident revolutionary of the zodiac, Aquarius is big on originality and reworking the system. With a focus on groups, progressive ideas, and innovation, this Sun placement is quite the humanitarian. As a fixed air sign, you kind of stand a little back from the crowd in order to take it all in. Your strength lies in your ability to understand the needs of the whole, which is knowledge that you use to rethink outdated, detrimental systems. You prefer clarity over emotional displays, as you don't just want to identify a problem: you want to fix it. Rationality and intellectual pursuits are both way up there on your list of favorite things. That's not to say you don't have emotions; you most certainly do! You tend to show your enthusiasm *after* you get what's going on.

Aquarians can be something of a wild card. You don't like doing things in the traditional fashion. You understand that just because things were always done one way, that doesn't make it the best way. And the beauty of it is, you usually *can* find a new, better system. Unnecessarily redundant or superfluous things drive you up a wall, as does misused authority and injustice. Aquarius is ruled by Uranus, which means you embrace visionary ideas and unconventional attitudes.

Naturally egalitarian, you're usually incredibly tolerant of other people. You can talk to just about anyone without judgment, because you're interested in understanding all viewpoints. This open-mindedness is actually pretty rare, and it draws people to you. You can be friends with folks even when you don't agree with their worldview, because your own personal values are so well defined. Honestly, you're an eccentric at heart; you love hearing from all walks of life. You're not threatened by people or ideas that are strange or unusual. You're smart as a whip, there's no denying it! But sometimes, your cool intellect can lend you an air of aloofness. Be careful of being too standoffish, only contributing logic or facts. You're a human being, and your heart is just as important as your head.

Sun in Pisces

The last zodiac sign in the astrological year, Pisces are usually old souls. Like all water signs, you have a well-developed sense of empathy, but in Pisces, this is kicked up to a nearly psychic level. For some reason, you feel like you just *get* the entire spectrum of the human experience. You feel what those around you are feeling, for better or for worse. Even the atmosphere of the room seeps into you! Adaptability is the name of the game for you, usually on a subconscious level. Unfortunately, this also means you can easily be swallowed by the emotions of others. You need time away from the demands of the world to rest and recharge. Pisces have a reputation for being daydreamers, but it's just your defense mechanism at work, protecting your beautiful, sensitive core from the ugliness of reality. Just be sure to check that your feet are still on the ground every so often.

Your symbol is two fish swimming in opposite directions, and you've probably felt that contradictory tug between fantasy and reality. This Sun placement constantly feels pulled in different directions. You want to try it all, to feel the breadth of the human experience. Good thing you're talented at just about anything! Still, it can be helpful for Pisces to focus on a distinct path. Set down intentions and stick to them. Without a goal in mind, you can end up swimming in circles, as you bounce from one thing to another, never getting anywhere.

As a mutable water sign, you're super flexible. You can easily adjust to fit whatever works best in your immediate surroundings. All that sensitivity and kindness make you quite the charmer when you want to be. You're probably great at parties. You can talk to anyone, and you'll go out of your way to help folks. Any kind of suffering or injustice you see engraves itself upon your heart. When it gets to be too much, you're known to just disappear for a while. Whether that means spacing out or getting lost in a book or video game, you need time to retreat into another world. Pisces need to be extra careful not to sink into any kind of addiction in their quest to escape. Boundaries are a big necessity for you fish folk. Your needs matter too!

Moon Signs

Ah, the lovely, ever-changing Moon! Is there anything else in our skies that just gives all the feels? The Moon has always been associated with the concepts of the subconscious, intuition, and hidden power. The lunar cycle has always had an influence on our lives—most notably our ocean tides, and also the recurring monthly phases and seasons. Ever heard it said that emotions run wild when the Moon is full? Or about someone "mooning" over someone else? It has always been believed that the phases of the Moon can affect the state of our emotions, and even cause madness or insanity. For example, look at the origins of the term *lunatic*. This stems from the Latin word *lunaticus,* which means being "moonstruck," or acting weird and being out of sorts. And the root word of *lunaticus*? Why, that's the Latin word *luna,* or Moon. The origin of these terms helps us understand that the Moon has been a symbol of our emotions, self-reflections, and mental state for centuries.

With all that history, it should come as no surprise that in the world of astrology, the Moon is all about our inner lives, our emotions, and our needs. Emotions and desires shift, just as the Moon changes shape every night. The Moon feels inherently more private, intimate, and vulnerable than the Sun. Think about how a conversation held on a sunny day feels in comparison to a whispered, moonlit heart-to-heart. For most people, the innermost desires of the heart are not shared with just anyone!

Your Moon sign takes your Sun sign energy and reflects it back through an emotional lens. This lens is different for everyone, which is why you can have, for instance, two Virgos with wildly different ways of moving through life. Everyone sees the world through their own emotional filter, made up of all their past experiences, personal values, fears, and connections. So, despite sharing a similar sense of self, two Virgos are likely to have developed different ways of processing their feelings and meeting their needs. They will react to identical circumstances in different ways, despite having a similar worldview. Your Moon sign has a huge impact on how you process your feelings, what you need to feel safe, and who you are when no one is looking. To be dramatic, your Moon sign is your soul's truest reflection.

Moon in Aries

Aries Moons are big on taking action, like, right now! This fiery Moon placement is all about living in the moment. You're basically the definition of a mover and shaker. It's kind of tough for you to wait around for things to happen, so much so that it makes you downright uncomfortable to be doing nothing. You feel most alive when you're facing down some challenge or jumping into a new project. Your desires flare hot, whether that's a new crush or a shirt you saw and just *had* to have right this second. With that said, if not managed well, all that fiery passion can burn itself out just as quickly as it ignited.

Long-term who? An Aries Moon is more of an instant gratification type of person. Hey, life is short, and you know it! You're usually very direct, with a strong desire to put yourself out there in the world. You tend to act on whims, and your natural independence means you have no trouble surging ahead of the crowd. You have no patience for mind games or manipulation. If you want something, you'll straight up say so. And honestly, you tend to get your way!

You normally exude self-confidence, whether you actually feel it or not. That inner passion shines through and draws people to you. Your emotional needs can kind of be like a hurricane, sweeping up everyone around you, whether they want it or not. Life is never dull around a lunar Aries!

Moon in Taurus

With the Moon in Taurus, you flourish when you're creating a life filled with all your favorite comforts. You know what you want, and you work hard to achieve it. Stability is huge for any Taurus placement. It's essential for you to have a comfortable, serene, and stable environment. You have no problem taking responsibility for yourself, especially as you grow older.

Taurus Moons place a high value on serenity and security. In the social realm, you're likely very tactful and sympathetic. You're someone people can rely on. Your steadiness is a natural quality that draws people to you. And man, oh man, do you know how to have fun! You always strive to make everything from a coffee date to a full-scale dinner the most pleasant, satisfying experience possible. You just like things to be nice! To that end, many lunar Taureans will go way out of their way to avoid chaotic situations and bad vibes.

Among the most sensual of the Moon signs, Taurus Moons tend to be rather romantic. After all, you have that beautiful stability mind-set. This Moon sign loves to be building something: their dream life, a big bank account, and rock-solid foundations in their relationships. When a Taurean Moon is committed, you can bet that they're in it for the long haul. You prefer to approach relationships with the idea of permanence firmly in mind. This desire to persevere is admirable, but it can be a danger when it goes too far. A Taurus Moon may end up stuck in a toxic cycle simply because it's familiar. Pay attention to your own needs too!

Moon in Gemini

Gemini energy is all about communication and knowledge, making this Moon placement a naturally witty and intelligent one. Your mind is a busy place! Ideas, opinions, facts, weird trivia . . . you've always got something racing through that brain, and you love to share it with the world. Energetic and enthusiastic, you likely have quite a diverse set of interests. It's not uncommon for a Gemini Moon to feel torn between their different "selves:" the introvert, who wants to learn everything and explore all the options, and the extrovert, who needs to share that information far and wide. You want to learn it all, explain it all, and do it all!

Lunar Geminis tend to have a constant need for contact and connectedness. They simply love talking to people and have quite the way with words. These Moons feel an immense sense of satisfaction when surrounded by friends, chatting about anything and everything. Your openness to others' ideas makes you a very tolerant friend. In fact, adaptability is one of your best traits! You're blessed with the sharp wit and intellect needed to be able to talk to just about anyone.

You live a work-in-progress life, mostly because you're always curious about what's coming. Gemini Moons are typically more scientifically minded, with a preference for a logical, systematic approach to things. You're pretty much amazing at analyzing things down to the finest details . . . including your own feelings and emotions. Of course, Gemini Moons *have* all the emotions of any other sign; they simply express them a little differently than others might expect. They'll take mental stimulation over emotional complications any day!

Moon in Cancer

Has anyone ever told you that you were very emotional? With your Moon in watery, intense Cancer, the chances of this are high. Cancer Moons tend to be very wrapped up in their own inner world. Your imagination is incredibly rich, and your emotional waters run deep. Like, unfathomably deep. Family, friends, lovers, enemies . . . your emotional connections are the pillars of your life. Cancer Moons approach everything from a perspective of long-lasting connection. You simply don't do superficial relationships.

Your superpower is your amazing sense of empathy. You genuinely want to do the best you can to help your loved ones, to make everyone around you feel happy and fulfilled. Obviously, this is a beautiful quality, but it can also lead to putting the needs of others before your own. Your well-being is just as important as everyone else's. Doing so much for others can lead to Cancer Moons feeling a bit taken for granted. When this happens, it might not be apparent to others right away. Not a fan of confrontation, these lunar natives prefer to drop hints or seek attention in rather indirect ways. An underdeveloped Cancer Moon can fall into reclusive or passive-aggressive patterns if they don't learn to confront life's inevitable conflicts. It's best to learn to set and honor your own emotional boundaries before getting to that point of frustration.

Cancer Moons, blessed with that empathy and emotional awareness, tend to be deeply attached to their memories. Nostalgia is an everyday fact of life for you.

You can dwell on the past like no other, feeling the emotions tied to your memories as if it happened yesterday. This is great when focused on good memories . . . and not so great when revisiting past hurts. After all, when someone hurts you once, who's to say it won't happen again? Trust is hard-earned with a Cancer Moon. Once they finally decide to invest, they cling to that sense of security and familiarity. Not thrilled with change, lunar Cancerians prefer the safety of their own space and routines, as it satisfies their deep need for peace and tenderness.

Moon in Leo

Enthusiastic, daring, and courageous, Leo Moons have a certain something special that draws others to them. While you don't necessarily *need* to be the center of attention, you still love to soak up the spotlight when you feel comfortable, surrounded by friends and family. Entertaining, funny, and creative as heck, you were born with an innate flair for drama. Leo Moons have a deep need to express themselves, to release all that natural creativity in some dramatic outlet. Depending on the rest of the chart, this can manifest in any number of ways, from their fashion choices to their career choices. No matter how a Leo Moon chooses to express themselves, they will thrive on praise and applause. After all, you are well aware that effort is the key to success, and you don't shy away from working for what you want! What's wrong with wanting your work to be recognized?

Leo Moons are given alternatively to emotional displays or sulking when they feel slighted or ignored, depending on the situation. Since Leo placements are hyperaware of external image and appearances, they prefer to avoid public spectacles. Expect more quiet sullenness in public, with the emotional drama saved for the comfort of home. The drama flares up hot but tends to burn out quickly. That emotional expressiveness goes both ways, luckily! When feeling happy and secure, you're more than willing to shower your loved ones with compliments and affection. It's very important to you to both share your love and to have your love reciprocated.

You feel most secure when showered in love and attention. Nothing wrong with that! You're already so likable that compliments and affection tend to come your way easily. Dealing with all the recognition may be a different story, however. You may have a somewhat complicated relationship with attention, whether it be losing yourself in the hype or feeling guilty about stealing the show. Many underdeveloped Leo Moons overindulge in the performance, losing sight of their true selves. There's also a danger of a superiority complex, because so many Leo Moons *are* truly gifted and ambitious. While they are rather fixed in their opinions, Leo Moons have a strong sense of integrity and justice. You place a high value on fairness and stick to your well-developed set of principles. With just about zero interest in deceit and pettiness, Leo Moons make extremely trustworthy friends.

Moon in Virgo

It's all about the details with this lunar placement! Virgo Moons feel most at peace when all the wrinkles are ironed out of, well, everything. Running errands? Organizing their space? Making the perfect cup of coffee? If a Virgo Moon can check it off their to-do list, they feel productive and happy. You're very realistic, with a preference for structure. Life feels best when everything is in its right place. Disorder and chaos? No, thank you! While a developed Virgo Moon can efficiently tackle unexpected chaos and create order, underdeveloped ones can instead become irate and aggressive when faced with disarray, tearing everything down.

That amazing instinct for taking care of the smallest details is one of your greatest strengths. You're the one other people come to when facing a seemingly insurmountable problem, because you tend to have invaluable advice. You're interested in every part of others' problems, and you have a solid practicality that many other people seem to lack. Plus, you love to be useful, so helping others truly gives you a sense of fulfillment. Added bonus: it gives you a chance to leave off worrying about your own problems for a while! You're not a fan of high-pressure situations, as you tend to overthink yourself into the ground when there's too much being thrown at you too fast.

That said, the idea of having everything "perfect" can also be a source of extreme stress for Virgo Moons. That ability to constantly refine things is truly admirable, especially when applied to making the world a better place. The danger lies in trying to force perfection on yourself, or on others around you. Humans are innately imperfect, and mistakes are a part of life. Don't beat yourself up! Turn your enthusiasm and desire for flawlessness toward something productive, like honing your variety of skills. Having your own small, daily rituals can also help you emotionally regulate, filtering out the clutter and self-criticisms.

Moon in Libra

With a strong Venus influence, Libra Moons truly resonate with everything that the Greek goddess of love and beauty represents. You have a deep desire to create things of beauty, to bring peace and balance to all things. Ugly things like injustice and conflict jar these lunar natives to the bone. After all, you believe things are more beautiful when brought into symmetry. Perceived flaws will bother the heck out of you until you can fix them. With your discerning eye comes some very high expectations. If you can't allow for human variety, you'll be searching for an impossible perfection all your life.

You apply the ideas of beauty and diplomacy to everything in life, including your surroundings, your words, and your relationships. It can be very difficult for you to deal with conflict, especially with the people you care for. Confrontation inevitably brings discord, however temporary, and you work hard to avoid that. A stressed, unbalanced Libra Moon may bend over backward trying to avoid any and all disagreement, ignoring their own needs and putting off any big decisions. As you grow, you recognize just how essential it is to care for yourself first, so you can be better for yourself and everyone around you.

Connections are vitally important to you. Life simply doesn't feel complete when you don't have someone around to share it with, whether that's a partner or your bestie. Luckily, you're pretty amazing at making people feel seen and loved!

Being charming and likeable is how you create safety and security in your life, and it invariably draws people to you. Libra Moons can be rather flirtatious—often without even trying—thanks to their ability to make someone feel like the most important person in the room. You're naturally talented at discovering the needs and motivations of others, which in turn actually helps you learn more about yourself in the long run.

Moon in Scorpio

Among the most intense and transformative of signs, Scorpio doesn't shy away from life's difficult moments. This Moon placement lends you some serious emotional depth. Still waters run deep, goes the saying, and your waters conceal quite a lot! Persevering, intriguing, and devoted, you see right through pretense. You're actually pretty good in high-pressure situations. No matter what life throws your way, you like to challenge yourself to overcome it. When it hits the fan, you're ready to test out just how strong you really are! Very resourceful, you prefer to tackle your own problems without any help. You'll work until you accomplish what you set out to do, with an intense dedication to the task.

As a water sign, you are blessed with emotional acuity. You can generally read other people's feelings with ease and have an uncanny ability to evoke intense emotion. You have a special presence that makes people want to rely on you. Chances are very high that people have spilled their deepest secrets to you, even if you just met them! Luckily, you're also amazingly trustworthy. Intuition is pretty much your top stat. You can rapidly pick up on the motivations of those around you. You just seem to know exactly how things are going to go down. You may even have felt as though you were psychic at times.

On a darker note, with the ability to see exactly where things are heading, Scorpio Moons may choose to simply close themselves off rather than deal with a sticky issue. One of this placement's greatest fears? Betrayal. To avoid being hurt, this watery placement may isolate themselves, diving deep into their comfort zone despite knowing full well that it isn't healthy behavior. Even the potential of a future disappointment can drag these lunar scorpions down into obsessive behaviors. They know that life doesn't always turn out rosy, and prefer to feel things out before diving in. In an underdeveloped Scorpio Moon, this can result in seemingly arbitrary "tests" of their loved ones. More developed Moon in Scorpio folks prefer to use their powers for good, forging incredibly deep bonds between themselves and other people.

Moon in Sagittarius

With the Moon in Sagittarius, you're a born adventurer! You have a deep need for independence and personal freedom. When you feel trapped or stagnant? That's pretty much the depths of hell for you. Sagittarius Moons have an unquenchable need for activity, for going out and interacting with all that the world has to offer. You're the type to nurture a lifelong love of learning, especially learning by experience. Energetic and adaptable, you want to go everywhere and try everything at least once. This applies to experiences of the mind as well as the body: Sagittarius Moons thrive when surrounded by mind-opening art, music, and conversation. You can spend hours talking about your wide and varied interests and come out feeling invigorated rather than drained.

One of the most beautiful qualities of a Sagittarius Moon is your natural sense of optimism. You tend to believe that everything will work out in the end. Your upbeat cheerfulness helps brighten up nearly any situation, drawing other people to you like moths to a flame. You know how to have fun! When you feel confident and secure, problems and obstacles barely even faze you. You know you can handle it. It's essential for a Sagittarius Moon to surround themselves with trustworthy people, as more devious types may try to take advantage of your desire to always see the good.

Sagittarius Moons are among the most free-spirited of all lunar placements. You are not big on planning things out.

Instead, you prefer to let things unfold naturally. "Winging it" is very much a valid strategy for you. The idea of a regular routine sends shivers down your spine. There's just so much to do and see in this life! You need to change up the scenery quite a bit, whether that's walking around a new neighborhood randomly or trying out deep-sea diving in another country. When life gets too tense (or too humdrum!), you feel a need to escape. That's not to say you won't come back; you will! You just need some time away to renew your optimistic spirit.

Moon in Capricorn

Steady, dependable, and competent, you're the epitome of the "Most Likely to Succeed" superlative! Being productive and reliable are way up there on the list of any Capricorn Moon's deepest needs. You set your aims high and work hard to accomplish those goals. In fact, "work hard" barely even scratches the surface; you're the type to put in *extreme* amounts of effort, despite the very real danger of burning yourself out. You don't just talk the talk; you walk the walk. Ideas are all well and good, but you want to see them backed up with action. You feel most fulfilled when you can see direct results of your efforts, as you place a high value on the tangible. For you, a perfect life is one where you feel worthwhile and respected.

Capricorn Moons were basically born with common sense and find it frustrating when other people don't share that sensibility. You prefer to approach things with a healthy sense of caution, whether that's your next career opportunity or a new relationship. It's part of your nature to protect yourself from manipulations and disappointments, so you need to get to know someone on a deeper level before you'll really open up. Even then, you keep some of your emotional depths locked away. Boundaries are of paramount importance to this Moon sign. There's nothing wrong with that! Healthy boundaries are absolutely essential in maintaining your inner peace in a life as busy as yours.

Strong-willed and self-reliant, Capricorn Moons feel most comfortable when they can control the situation. Cool, calm, and collected is the look of choice for you, regardless of whether you actually feel that way or not. You're not particularly thrilled with messy emotional displays, preferring to keep emotions on a careful lock. This doesn't mean you don't have emotions. Quite the opposite. You can be prone to mood swings and dark emotions that may never be shared with the world. Many Capricorn Moons hide their sensitivity behind a cool, sarcastic mask. This need to keep things under control can cause this lunar placement to be very hard on themselves. Undeveloped Moon in Capricorn folks may force themselves to go without, denying themselves much-needed care and attention to try to feel secure and in control. It's important to balance your desire to accomplish everything with the self-care necessary for emotional and mental well-being. Sure, it might feel easier to focus on your very real obligations, but it's ultimately going to be more rewarding to prioritize your own happiness.

Moon in Aquarius

With your Moon in Aquarius, you're sure to stand apart from the crowd! This airy placement has a powerful need for independence. Many lunar Aquarians grow up feeling a bit different from everyone else. The happiest ones tend to be those who embrace that uniqueness, leaning in and relishing being the "weird" one. After all, who wants to be boring? This outlook can mean that you spend a lot of time feeling like you're on the outside looking in. It's not always a bad place to be, especially for someone blessed with your sharp intellect and curiosity. You may even consider yourself a student of human nature; Aquarius Moons notice quite a bit and are very interested in figuring out *why* people do what they do. You find it fascinating to analyze other people's behavior and emotions.

It's not always readily apparent in the Moon placement, but Aquarius is a fixed sign, giving you a bit of a stubborn streak. You're secretly very sensitive to criticism, as you have an inner anxiety that eats at you in social situations. No one wants to look stupid or feel rejected, but this goes double for you! To hide these fears, Aquarius Moons might just double down on any behavior they get called out on. You can also become very cold and uncompromising when confronted. You expect everyone around you to be just as independent and detached as you are, which can be maddening for the more expressive signs. Happily, this also means you're very tolerant of other people's quirks and never try to stifle or change your loved ones. You rightly refuse to change for anyone, as you will never ask anyone to change for you!

Aquarius Moons thrive when allowed time and space to indulge their boundless curiosity. Idealistic, progressive, and visionary, you value ideas over feelings. Lunar Aquarians love to learn about pretty much everything and can be counted on to find a weird-yet-amazing solution to most problems. You truly want to make the world a better place, and more power to you for it! You're a great friend who makes the extra effort to include everyone. However, with all that humanitarian influence from Aquarius, it's not uncommon for this placement to decide that some of the baser human emotions—like anger, envy, and fear—should be ignored. You find it useful to approach everything from a logical viewpoint, including emotional situations. Unfortunately, not only does this make you come across as rather cold and aloof, but it also alienates you from a lot of human experiences. It's important for you to take time alone to reflect and feel secure enough to tackle these kinds of challenges. Aquarius Moons create a safe place for themselves through detachment.

Moon in Pisces

With your Moon in compassionate Pisces, you're basically intuition incarnate. Most Pisces Moons live their lives based on what *feels* right, relying heavily on the vibe of a person or situation. Empathy is the name of the game with a Pisces Moon. As the last sign in the zodiac, Pisces has a bit of each astrology sign in them, giving you an uncanny ability to truly understand other people and to break down boundaries. Incredibly understanding and accepting, you've probably had people open up to you unprompted. You always want to see the best in everyone and everything. It's kind of your thing: transforming the mundane into something magical. You prefer to live in a rose-colored daydream rather than drown in the ugliness of the real world.

Pisces Moons trust easily. In early life, it's very likely you thought people were inherently good. Maybe you still believe that! Unfortunately, this also means that until they experience more of life, Pisces Moons are rather easily manipulated. It's very easy for you to get swept up in the suffering of others. Your heartstrings are right out in the open, ready to be tugged upon by anyone with a sob story. You simply don't understand why anyone would have evil or selfish intentions. Anyone with this placement would do well to learn to establish real, definite boundaries—and stick to them. Luckily, as you develop your intuitive skills, it becomes easier to distinguish between the manipulators and those who actually need your help.

Imaginative and drawn to the arts, you're always coming up with new dreams and ideas. Unfortunately, Moon in Pisces folks may forget to apply some realism to these great thoughts. It can be difficult

for them to buckle down to actually make headway or to deal with unexpected complications. Day-to-day practicalities? No, thank you! You might come across as a bit absent-minded or spacey, but checking out of reality is just your natural self-care technique. Without time and space to daydream and mellow out, lunar Pisces are easily overloaded with life's demands. When this happens, a physical or mental escape is absolutely essential for you. There's not always even a specific reason you seek out solitude; it may simply *feel* right. It's how you regulate your emotions and renew your sense of confidence in yourself. Given time to gather your strength, you're ready to get back out there!

Rising Signs

You've gotten to know your Sun and your Moon signs. The last part of the "Big Three"? Your Rising sign, or your Ascendant. Your Ascendant is the sign that was quite literally coming over the horizon the moment you took your first breath. Not to freak you out or anything, but this is the one that needs you to be as exact as possible with your birth time! Rising signs change every two hours or so, which is why precision is so important. Minutes can make the difference sometimes. The more exact your birth time, the more accurately your Rising sign will reflect you.

So what exactly *is* your Ascendant? It's basically how you interact with the world: the way you look at things and the way others see you. It's the first impressions sign, essentially, because when people first meet you, this is the mask they see. The rest of your birth chart is tucked up behind the Ascendant, revealed only as people get to know you better. Fun fact: way back in the day, when people asked your sign, they didn't mean Sun sign; they meant your Rising sign! These are the most readily apparent traits you show, after all. They relate to your fashion choices, general appearance, and even health. Keep in mind that your health as a whole is incredibly intricate and important to maintain. We note the traditional body parts ruled by each Ascendant more for fun than anything else and because they are weirdly accurate most of the time. Still, you really shouldn't base

your health choices on your zodiac signs. Take good care of your entire beautiful self—mind, body, and soul. And remember to always ask your doctor before doing anything that affects your health.

If you calculated your birth chart with the correct date, place, and time of birth, you should know your Ascendant. Find your Rising sign in the next part and get all the juicy details!

Aries Rising

Warrior vibes right here! With powerful Aries on the horizon, you were born ready. Ready for what, you ask? Honestly, the answer to that is . . . pretty much anything! You're all about activating potential. Aries Rising folks are not afraid to speak up or to step up. You're never short on courage. You're the type to ask for forgiveness, not permission. How would things get done, otherwise? You rush into action headfirst, consequences be damned. While this can obviously come with some problems, they're usually nothing you can't handle. Aries Rising is a resilient sign, blessed with perseverance and boundless energy.

You come across as bold, outspoken, and straight-up fearless. No one would ever mistake you for a shrinking violet. You crave activity, and you want it *now*! Patience is not a strong suit with this Ascendant. Aries Risings typically move fast, preferring to be first even in the smallest of things. In your eyes, everything is better when done as quickly as possible, even just walking to the store! You're likely to be described as extremely independent, thanks to your ability to get things done from an early age. Don't be afraid to ask for help when you need it, though. That takes just as much courage as going at it alone.

Since you're pretty much bursting at the seams with fiery passion, it's important that you apply your energy to the right causes. Without a direction, Aries Rising can explode at the smallest provocation, doing serious harm to relationships, or even to themselves. Use your powers for good.

Aries traditionally rules the head and the face. For an Ascendant, this relates to your appearance. We're willing to bet you have a beautiful, expressive face, with a quick smile. It also means you may have issues in this area of your body, such as headaches, rashes, or eye problems. Take care of yourself, darling!

Your keywords are competition, instinct, and presence.

Taurus Rising

You're all about that relaxed glamour. Things have to feel just right for you! There's no rushing a Taurus Rising. Firmly entrenched in your ways, you're not specially big on change. You need time to feel it all out, to probe a situation with all five of your senses. Taurus is a fixed sign, after all. That famous staying power is usually coupled with an unwillingness to step out of your comfort zone. And why not? Your comfort zone is likely to be a beautifully curated space, thanks to your discerning eye. Creating a stable place, filled with all your creature comforts? That's a life essential for you. Thank goodness you have the tenacity needed to build that life!

You come across as peaceful, mellow, and chill. People are drawn to the sense of stability you offer. You thrive when you feel safe and secure, and so does everyone around you. By giving yourself and others a place to feel safe, you create the opportunity to truly enjoy each other's company, along with all the pleasures life has to offer. Because you're never in short supply of pleasure! Life is meant to be lived. You understand that planting your garden now will allow you to reap the rewards in the future and nurture more and more growth over time. That's the beauty of your slow and steady determination.

With your eye on the prize, you're always working with future abundance in mind. Be careful of trying to force the world to work according to your schedule. This is a benevolent universe, but you must trust the process. You cannot force it; you must adjust to it. You can and will persevere!

Taurus rules the neck, throat, and shoulders. Many Taurus Rising individuals are blessed with a graceful neck and charming voice! However, they may encounter issues with sore throats, achy or stiff necks, and upper body sensitivities. Take good care of your neck. Gently stretching goes a long way.

Your keywords are sensuality, willpower, and persistence.

Gemini Rising

Your friendly, vibrant energy is downright infectious! For you, life is all about communication and connection. You're driven to learn everything you possibly can, then spread that information far and wide. You just don't have a pause button. You're always in motion, teasing out more facts and details and stories. The beauty of your mercurial energy lies in your ability to look at things from just about any angle. You're very comfortable navigating mysteries and contradictions because you know there's no such thing as complete certainty. You're blessed with the charisma and cleverness needed to persuade just about anyone of anything.

You come across as interesting, agile, and clever. You're restless and quick-witted, and changing it up is kind of your thing. Gemini is ruled by Mercury, after all, the planet of language, messages, and intellect. Your curiosity is pretty much insatiable! This makes for a truly fascinating individual. You love to make sense of the world, which is why you approach life from a more objective position than more emotionally driven Rising signs. You're not too big on weighty responsibilities or irrational emotional outbursts. You need the freedom to move around and experience new things!

Gemini traditionally rules the arms and chest. And no, it's not an accident that this includes the lungs, arms, and hands, which all have two parts to them. Gemini's symbol is the twins, after all.

Many of these Ascendants are known for talking with their hands and using expressive gestures. Gemini Risings might need to watch out for problems in these areas though, such as anxious fidgeting, lung issues, or arthritis.

Your keywords are variety, information, and curiosity.

Cancer Rising

Remembering the little things? Sensitive to the vibes of things? Taking care of everyone? Check, check, and check. Cancer Risings are natural caretakers, driven to strengthen emotional connections and create a place of safety for themselves and their loved ones. Protected by their tough outer shell, this placement is among the most sensitive of Ascendants. Like their symbol, the crab, Cancer Rising folks prefer to work their way carefully into new situations, sliding into things sideways in their own good time. You're always there for other people and can handle the tough moments in life. You seem to just intuitively understand people's needs and people tend to come to you for comfort and help.

You come across as gentle, protective, and caring. People are drawn to your beautiful, nurturing energy. You encourage others to grow and flourish when they're surrounded by your powerful glow of support. You have an incredible connection to the past, placing a lot of value on family and your roots. It's hard for you to see things objectively sometimes, as you approach everything from a very personal point of view. Your moods are prone to change as the mood around you shifts.

Cancer rules the stomach and breasts, regardless of gender. These body parts symbolize nourishment and support, which Cancer Risings excel at both literally and figuratively. When overwhelmed with emotions or stress, Cancer Risings may suffer from indigestion or overindulgence. Let go of the things you can't control!

Your keywords are nurture, memory, and connection.

Leo Rising

All the world's a stage! With a flair for the dramatic and an unquenchable thirst for life, you tend to stand out. Leo Risings have an innate sense of self-awareness and are hyperaware of the image they project. Driven by that sunny Leo energy, you thrive when you're given the freedom to express your creativity, ideally as the star of the show. Leo Rising folks may lean toward the bossy when they're really passionate about something, but most just want to make sure things are the best they can be. When your pride is wounded, you're prone to lash out. Still, it's rare for you to hold a grudge. You prefer to leave the past in the past and enjoy the present moment.

You come across as optimistic, high-spirited, and confident. You have a great deal of pride in everything you do. Leo Risings might be accused of being rather vain, but they just like to impress! No one would ever mistake you for timid, and you like it that way. People are drawn to your radiant magnetism and your ability to reflect the best of a person back at them. You likely go to great lengths to present a good face to the world, hiding your more vulnerable moments away in private.

The heart and spine are ruled by Leo. All that strength and passion! Leo Risings tend to stand up tall and embrace activitie that get the blood pumping. If they push themselves too far, however, they run the risk of burnout. Watch out for back pain, blood issues, and exhaustion.

Your keywords are performance, fun, and creativity.

Virgo Rising

Practical and driven to make things as perfect as possible, Virgo Risings are in a league all their own. No sign pays attention to detail like a Virgo, which is a huge asset when you're engrossed in a project. Blessed with impressive analytical and observational powers, you can always tell when something isn't right. Refinement is your gift. Whether it's an upset friend or a work project in disarray, you've always been able to see just what needs tweaking to make things better. Virgo Risings will work diligently to put life together just right for themselves and everyone around them, smoothing out the wrinkles and dropping dead weight. That exacting nature can put some off at times, but the right people will recognize the Virgo desire to help others is what's driving that critical manner.

You come across as composed, professional, and dignified. You have a playing-it-cool perfectionist vibe, whether you feel that way or not on the inside. Many Virgo Risings keep their rather neurotic tendencies hidden, presenting a reserved face to the world. You need time to warm up to people, but once you've opened your heart to someone, you are all in. You'll go out of your way to help a loved one in need. You have the rare ability to remain calm in the face of chaos.

Virgo traditionally rules the digestive system and intestines. It might not sound the most glamorous, but these essential organs do a lot of unseen work, supporting the rest of the body. Sound like a certain meticulous sign? Virgo Risings should take extra care in nourishing their digestive systems. While it's easier said than done, these Ascendants should avoid overthinking and excessive worrying, as that can also lead to digestive issues.

Your keywords are detail, devotion, and reliability.

Libra Rising

Friendly and magnetic, you were born to captivate others! With a love for all things fair, balanced, and symmetrical, you strive to keep things harmonious. You're always on alert for little social cues, ready to jump in and make things right if it's within your power. You make an amazing host, with your ability to charm coupled with your innate sense of taste. The home of a Libra Rising is typically a work of art all on its own. Libra is ruled by Venus, after all! You thrive when you can fit everything together just so, reconciling all the discordant notes of the world into a perfect, peaceful balance.

You come across as pleasant, enchanting, and accommodating. Your desire to make everything as lovely and poised as possible is driven by your innate desire for balance. Libra Risings hate to see others bullied or left out. These are the peacemakers of the zodiac, the kind of folks who prize cooperation, compromise, and calm. You know just how to liven up a conversation, defuse a confrontation, and keep everyone moving toward a common goal. Libra Risings tend to get what they want, without the other party even realizing they've been steered a certain way.

Libra rules the kidneys, skin, and booty. All these body parts are responsible for maintaining balance within and without the body. Libra Ascendants of any gender tend to be rather attractive, most obviously in their lovely, often sensitive, skin.

However, when their internal chemistry is out of whack, especially due to stress or poor nutrition, these folks can suffer from skin ailments and lower back pain. Your body's needs are important! Don't neglect yourself while caring for other people.

Your keywords are charm, relationships, and balance.

Scorpio Rising

That intensity! With an unmatchable determination and a formidable hidden-depths vibe, you make quite the impression. Without saying a word, Scorpio Rising people can dominate a room. This can be a bit polarizing for others, but whether loved or hated, there's no ignoring a Scorpio Ascendant. Whatever your other placements, this watery Rising has the rare ability to see through the pretense, feeling out what's really going on with a person or situation. Your gut reactions are rarely wrong. You're driven to find the truth underlying everything and everyone.

You come across as powerful, private, and alluring. Your magnetism lies in your ability to transform. People are drawn to your unspoken sense of potency. You recognize the power and potential in change, despite the pain that often accompanies it. Scorpio Risings, on their eternal path toward truth, are not afraid to look darkness and discomfort in the face. Good thing you're also blessed with quite the deep well of fortitude and tenacity! You know how to achieve what you set out to do, no matter the obstacles. Be careful of turning all that intensity in on yourself. Self-sabotage might look like taking control, but it really just smothers your capabilities.

Scorpio rules, what else, but the reproductive system. We know, it's a bit of a cliché, but think about it this way: sex is ultimately an act of transformation and creation. Scorpios excel at creating magic from the places both hidden and taboo. Watch out for issues in this area, as well as hormonal imbalances.

Your keywords are power, mystery, and resilience.

Sagittarius Rising

Always on the move, you bring your trademark enthusiasm to, like, everything. A born optimist, you're always looking to new horizons. Sagittarius's symbol is the centaur, shooting an arrow into the future. Sagittarius Ascendants are driven to seek, to discover. You likely have a lifelong love of learning, and you don't shy away from sharing what you know. In fact, you might be just the tiniest bit guilty o' oversharing your opinions on, well, just about everything. You're not trying to be a know-it-all, though; it's more that you realize knowledge moves the world in the right direction. Many Sagittarius Ascendants are on a lifelong spiritual journey and simply love life! You're always pouring truth and compassion into the world, and it's a beautiful thing.

You come across as enthusiastic, restless, and hopeful. Sagittarius Rising folks tend to have a lot of faith in the future, in what's just around the next corner. You're not known for taking anything slow. You don't shy away from taking risks. Always the optimist, you're willing to run straight toward the unknown, so it's a good thing that your natural Jovian luck is usually there to help you land on your feet. You have an unquenchable desire to discover new things and cannot tolerate any restrictions on your freedom. And oh my gosh, are you hilarious! Sagittarius Risings maintain a great sense of humor, even in the darkest of days. You just trust that the universe has your back, so your thoughts rarely linger on disappointments or defeats.

Sagittarius traditionally rules the hips and thighs. The celestial archer must be able to move around, right? How else will you stand up tall and run toward the next big thing? Without regular stretching and movement, Sagittarius Rising folks can face issues and tension in these areas. Make sure you extend your desire to explore to your physical routine!

Your keywords are freedom, energy, and adventure.

Capricorn Rising

The CEO vibe is strong in Capricorn Risings! With a knack for putting things to their best use, greatness is pretty much your thing. It helps that you're incredibly determined to chase down your goals, smart as a whip, and motivated as hell. You know what you want. When you set your sights on something, you chart the best course to reach that point. You're able to see just how to get the wheels going, in the most efficient way possible. Hard work doesn't faze a Capricorn Rising; in fact, they tend to thrive on it. Sometimes this can be taken to an unhealthy extreme, as stressed Capricorn Ascendants may deny themselves much-needed rest, rejecting any pleasure in life until harsh conditions are met. Remember to stop and enjoy the life you're creating!

You come across as mature, competent, and pragmatic. Capricorn Risings are thinkers, always planning the next phase of their lives. These folks are proud of their sense of responsibility, approaching life with innate poise. Capricorn Risings appreciate the value of hard-won wisdom, utilizing all their life lessons to accomplish great things. This also makes you an awesome teacher and natural leader. With your ability to organize everything and everyone to work at peak efficiency, you and your team can tackle just about any project. It helps that you have a great sense of dry humor, which you use to keep others engaged and morale high.

Capricorn rules the bones, knees, teeth, and joints. With all that focus on structure and support, you can see where the association came from. On the plus side, Capricorn Risings tend to have beautiful bone structure and great posture! However, these Ascendants are also prone to stiff joints, arthritis, and orthopedic issues. Take your vitamins!

Your keywords are longevity, caution, and determination.

Aquarius Rising

Independence looks amazing on you! Forget tradition and conformity; you prefer to think outside the box and go your own way. Aquarius Risings often go through life feeling like they're a bit different. You're blessed with a keenly observant mind, so being on the outside can be a bit of a vantage point for you! You're able to see things from a unique perspective, free from the usual blind spots someone stuck in an emotional whirlwind may have. You instinctively understand the way things work, and you thrive when finding a way to make them even better. With an altruistic drive, you focus your efforts more on broad humanitarian causes than on individual crises. Aquarius Rising folks have no time for narrow-minded views or emotional manipulators and have no problem making that clear.

You come across as unique, savvy, and friendly. People gravitate to both your fascinating personality and your tolerance for different opinions and ideas. Aquarius Risings tend to have a large social circle of acquaintances and a much smaller group of close friends. Aquarius Risings are naturally innovative, with the typical air sign intellect and the not-so-typical unswerving determination. This combination can feel a bit cold and calculating at times. Luckily, most Aquarius Ascendants come to understand the value of balancing that cool logic with emotion.

Aquarius traditionally rules the calves, shins, and circulatory system. Like blood moving through the body and sustaining all the other functions, Aquarius Risings circulate ideas. Aquarius Ascendants should pay special attention to their overall vascular health, as well as the state of their lower legs. Your health is always important!

Your keywords are intelligence, individuality, and perspective.

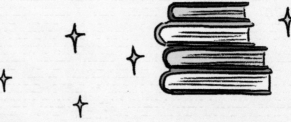

Pisces Rising

Are you psychic? Because you just always seem to know how others are feeling, despite your rather dreamy demeanor. Pisces Risings can pick up on just about everything, including other personas. One day you might be reserved and quiet, only to show up as a lively chatterbox the next. Pisces Ascendants are the type to walk a little different after watching a movie, they fall into a new character so easily. You gently refuse to be pinned down, simply drifting away from both harsh reality and tough decisions. Your inner life is incredibly rich, as you use it to escape real life whenever necessary. Others might sometimes see you as a bit of a space case because you tend to have your head in the clouds so often. Plans? Structure? Not really your thing. With all that watery Pisces influence, you prefer to move through life by how things *feel,* free to soak up whatever experiences you end up swimming into.

You come across as peaceful, gentle, and likeable. Maybe it's the compassionate way you approach others, but even the most closed-off people can open up before your soft emotional touch. You've probably had people come to you when they're at their lowest, seeking the healing your open heart and bottomless empathy provide. There are two things to watch out for here, our dear Pisces Rising: offering help when someone isn't ready, and giving away too much of yourself. Both problems stem from your intense desire to soothe suffering, but healthy boundaries are always essential, especially for you. You have to take care of yourself before you can take care of others!

Pisces rules the feet, toes, and endocrine system. The last sign of the zodiac, Pisces are said to carry a little of all the other signs. Well, in case you didn't know, the foot is linked to almost every other part of the body via pressure points. As an added bonus, many Pisces Risings are amazing dancers! Watch out for foot-related ailments and hormonal imbalances.

Your keywords are intuition, understanding, and compassion.

Chapter 2

Practical

Now that you're equipped with your birth chart and an understanding of your personal planets, it's finally time to jump into some astrology fun! Chapter 1 was the Astrology 101 class, and guess what? You've graduated! You're out in the real world of pop astrology now. You're ready to start using your new understanding of the zodiac out in the wide world of astrology.

To get used to zodiac-speak, we're going to take a look at the more practical side of things first. How can you actually talk about astrology signs in the real world? What little mannerisms always seem to define one sign? What's just a stereotype, and where does that perceived image come from? Just like learning any new language, you should immerse yourself in it on a personal level. Learn to see what's just oh-so-Pisces about you. Recognize your Sagittarius bestie's guilty pleasures. You'll soon be ready to whip out the astrology facts whenever needed.

For the rest of this book, we suggest having screenshots of your own birth chart, and, if you can wrangle them, charts of your friends and family! Especially if you're just starting out in astrology, having them for reference just makes it a lot easier to use the next few chapters.

We'll be saying to check certain signs for each of the sections that follow. You might be wondering why some say to check the Sun and not the Moon or Rising, or whatever combination it may be. Some sections are more generalized and don't touch on the more emotional side.

These will point more toward your Sun, and sometimes your Rising. You should check your Sun in every situation because that *is* your core identity.

When there's a bit more of an emotionally driven section? That's when your Moon comes into play more strongly. Sections that refer to how you might feel or react to something? You'll want to check your Moon. Remember, the Moon deals with emotions and stability.

Rising signs refer to your external self, the way you project yourself to others, so you'd always want to check that placement in a social context. Anytime we're talking about stuff like first impressions, fashion choices, and your skills, you'll want to check your Rising sign.

There's nothing stopping you from checking all of your Big Three, though! Everyone expresses their placements in a unique way, so get familiar with all of them. Eventually, you'll learn what feels right to you.

Positives and Negatives

There's a whole spectrum of traits associated with each zodiac sign, ranging from the under-evolved (or immature) to the evolved (or mature). You'll probably relate to traits on both sides, depending on the day. It's okay, we all have our ups and downs!

Check your Sun and Moon signs.

Aries

Positives:

- Go-getter attitude
- Doesn't need approval
- Trusting those instincts

Negatives:

- Literally zero patience
- Everything is a competition
- Risky and impulsive behavior

Taurus

Positives:

Truly the most reliable

Loves sharing with loved ones

Gets those damn results

Negatives:

- Materialistic to a fault
- Values comfort over growth
- Would die before asking for help

Gemini

Positives:

Truly down for anything

Always knows what to say

Charismatic and fun

Negatives:

- Too chaotic for their own good
- Either totally clingy or totally distant
- Blind to the consequences of their actions

Cancer

Positives:

Airtight, healthy boundaries

Takes care of others with
no expectations

Actively strives for a harmonious life

Negatives:

- Tries to fix others and ignores
  their own issues
- Tends to be fake-nice
- Wallows in past mistakes

Leo

Positives:

- Leader of the self-love club
- A living muse
- Will defend their friends to the ends of the Earth

Negatives:

- Constantly fishing for validation
- Rejects opposing opinions
- Drama level: unparalleled

Virgo

Positives:

- Creates order from chaos
- Leveling up themselves and their friends
- Appreciates and notices the small things

Negatives:

- Focuses on what's missing rather than what they have
- Insane amounts of self-doubt
- Values perfection too much

Libra

Positives:

- Amazing people skills
- Stands up to injustice
- Cultivates a more beautiful world

Negatives:

- Major personal boundary issues
- Bases their self-worth on other people's opinions
- Avoids conflict and ends up tolerating toxic people

Scorpio

Positives:

- Uses past trauma to transform and grow
- Highly tuned intuition
- Major healing vibes

Negatives:

- Can't move beyond past grudges
- Ruled by their wild emotions
- Hides their emotions until they lash out

Sagittarius

Positives:

- Uses their honesty and conviction for good
- Balances freedom and commitment
- Truly optimistic AF

Negatives:

- Rudeness disguised as "honesty"
- "Other people's opinions? Nah, I'm good."
- Runs from responsibility at top speed

Capricorn

Positives:

- Goals: attained. Dreams: achieved
- Respectful and respected
- Ready and willing to tackle any obstacle

Negatives:

- Secretly doubts themselves constantly
- Unhealthy fixation on working
- Difficulty expressing emotions

Aquarius

Positives:

- Genuinely seeks to better people's lives
- Thinks through stressful situations clearly
- Has a unique approach to life

Negatives:

- Struggles to handle emotional situations
- Contrarian just for the hell of it
- Feels like an outsider

Pisces

Positives:

- Famously compassionate
- Empathetic while maintaining boundaries
- Makes friends left and right

Negatives:

- Some love to play the martyr while others love to play the savior
- Retreats at the first sign of conflict
- Sinks into melancholy

Two Types of People

There are two types of people . . . and of each sign! We break down the usual zodiac typecasts into two groups here. Maybe your fiery energy is tempered by some water vibes, making you less of the typical hotheaded Aries, or you have some earth energy keeping your reckless Gemini nature under control. So, the question is, are you more of a Type 1 or a Type 2?

Check your Sun and Rising signs.

Aries

Type 1:

- Ultimate ride-or-die bestie
- Mind games? Never heard of 'em!
- Bossy babe vibes

Type 2:

- Sees the best even in the worst people
- Has pretty much zero patience
- Optimistic softie

Taurus

Type 1:

- Expert-level foodie
- Binge-watching Netflix between naps
- Replies to a text two days later

Type 2:

- Killer fashion sense
- Lives in a luxurious jungle of houseplants
- Watch out for that temper

Gemini

Type 1:

- Mood swings galore
- Annoyed by dumb people
- Hilarious sense of humor

Type 2:

- Social chameleon
- No one is ever bored around them
- Simultaneously offended and amused by Gemini roast memes

Cancer

Type 1:

- Animal whisperer
- Cries and blames it on the Moon
- Will do anything for loved ones

Type 2:

- Super sassy
- Mess with crab-o, get a stab-o
- Innate creative abilities

Leo

Type 1:

- Living the "lead role" lifestyle
- Can't take a joke
- All publicity is good publicity

Type 2:

- Generous to a fault
- Always down to chill with friends
- Insecure but hides it well

Virgo

Type 1:

- Stress cleaning at 3 a.m.
- Organization gives them life
- Low-key nature lover

Type 2:

- Human lie detector
- Hidden wild side
- Resistant to change

Libra

Type 1:

- Thrives on a good debate
- Kinda petty, to be honest
- That CONFIDENCE!

Type 2:

- Obsessed with live music
- Just wants everyone to get along
- That Libra indecisiveness

Scorpio

Type 1:

- "Your secret is safe with me"
- Sex appeal to the max
- Brooding intensifies

Type 2:

- Low-key sarcastic as hell
- Intimidation is my superpower
- "My trust issues have trust issues"

Sagittarius

Type 1:

- Dreams of #vanlife
- "I want to break free"
- Stranger to moderation

Type 2:

- Born comedian
- That famous Sagittarius honesty
- Inappropriate laughter

Capricorn

Type 1:

- Honey making money
- Refuses to be vulnerable
- The name of the game: extreme sarcasm

Type 2:

- Old soul
- Like, the nicest person in the world
- Stressed about every mistake since 2012

Aquarius

Type 1:

- Brainstorming genius
- Feelings? I haven't felt those in years
- CATS

Type 2:

- Ready to save the world
- Aliens are groovy
- #unpopularopinions

Pisces

Type 1:

- Empathizes with all living things
- Doesn't judge until they try it
- Lives with a hint of existential dread

Type 2:

- Enjoys a good nature walk
- Smarter than they seem
- Martyr complex

Stereotypes vs. Reality

Every sign gets stuck with some of the same stereotypes over and over. Time to debunk some of them! These stereotypes stem from an actual trait of each sign, usually taken to a bit of an extreme. Yeah, we know, there are always going to be generalizations about astrology signs, because they're such broad categories. But try to see where it comes from. Flex your astrological knowledge! The more you learn about astrology, the more you realize just how important everything in your chart is.

Check your Sun and Rising signs.

Aries

Stereotype:

- Low-key ready to brawl 24/7
- Extra impulsive
- Super bossy and rude

Reality:

- Actually knows their limits
- Believes life is an adventure
- Tells it like it is

Taurus

Stereotype:

- Only cares about food
- Spends money like water
- Stubborn and won't give anything new a chance

Reality:

- Sensory experiences make life worth living
- Loves to treat everyone
- Fears losing their sense of stability

Gemini

Stereotype:

- Never stops talking
- Wild and unpredictable
- Multiple personalities

Reality:

- Wants to share their passions
- Down to try it all
- Slips into the vibe of the room effortlessly

Cancer

Stereotype:

- Ultra-emotional crybaby
- Boring "mom" friend
- Super soft and vulnerable

Reality:

- Actually has great control of their emotions
- Deeply protective, nurturing energy
- Possesses truly impressive determination

Leo

Stereotype:

- Self-obsessed drama queen
- Totally sure of themselves
- Needs constant love and affection

Reality:

- Actually their friends' biggest cheerleader
- Very aware of how they're perceived
- Gives tons of love to other people

Virgo

Stereotype:

- Antisocial with impossible standards
- Hyper-organized robots
- Perfectionist energy

Reality:

- Tries to help loved ones be the best they can be
- Copes with nervous energy by controlling their space
- Puts care into the details

Libra

Stereotype:

- Wishy-washy and can't commit
- All about the drama
- All wrapped up in the opinions of other people

Reality:

- Considers all sides and can compromise
- Prefers harmony and balance
- Truly wants the best for everyone

Scorpio

Stereotype:

- Incredibly intense and overbearing
- Obsessed with death, sex, and power
- Fueled by slights and grudges

Reality:

- Feels their feelings on an incredibly deep level
- Shines light on the darker aspects of humanity
- Processes trauma in order to grow

Sagittarius

Stereotype:

- Positive and upbeat all the time
- Blunt and tactless
- Terrified of commitment

Reality:

- Hides their true feelings behind a happy façade
- Strong enough to speak the truth
- Wants relationships with room for change and growth

Capricorn

Stereotype:

- Total workaholic
- All about money and control
- Emotionless and hates having fun

Reality:

- Craves tangible results of their labors
- Worried about security
- Legit the funniest people

Aquarius

Stereotype:

- Detached and hard to relate to
- Rebel without a cause
- Weird loner obsessed with aliens

Reality:

- Just takes their time opening up
- Strong sense of personal values
- Actually great at making friends

Pisces

Stereotype:

- Addicted to their vices
- Sleepy, daydreaming ditz
- Softies who can't stand up for themselves

Reality:

- An accomplished escapist
- Prefers beautiful ideals over negativity
- Emotionally strong from carrying everyone else's baggage

Compatibility

Whether it's a bestie or a life partner, it's just the best feeling to find someone you totally click with! Some signs just vibe with each other better than others because they share similar ways of interacting with the world, or value the same things. Compatibility is a crazy deep topic, honestly. There's so much at play with just one individual! Adding more complex people to the equation? It gets deep, fast.

So, because compatibility is such an in-depth topic, this section is going to be just a little different from the rest in this book. Relationships are never set in stone. Friendship or romantic, they are constantly evolving as people grow and change. If your relationship is newer, you should compare Sun and Rising compatibility since those are the more recognizable traits of a person. Think first impressions and initial attraction. As you get to know a person better, the Moon comes more strongly into play. Moon signs are the emotional side of your soul, remember, and human relationships are obviously big on emotion.

Ready for the unusual part? We're also going to ask you to check back on that birth chart you generated and find your Venus and Mars placements. Why? Well, if you're looking at how you vibe with a partner in a romantic relationship, these placements are pretty dang important! Venus signs are all about love and beauty and tell you what kind of person you find attractive. Mars signs deal with aggression and sexual drive. You can see why these are essential elements to consider in compatibility! Check your compatibility in our handy chart.

NOTE

As we said, compatibility can go *deep*. Like, all the way out to the edge of our solar system deep. That's when you get more into synastry. Synastry is usually practiced by overlaying two peoples' birth charts and studying the similarities between placements, as well as any aspects, or angles, made between those placements. Yeah, this gets *very* involved. When you really want to look into how a relationship is supported and challenged, get the birth dates and times for both people and calculate a synastry chart!

Check your (and another person's) Sun, Moon, Venus, and Mars signs.

	Aries ♈	Taurus ♉	Gemini ♊	Cancer ♋	Leo ♌	V...
Aries ♈	♥	♥	♥	♥	♥	♥
Taurus ♉	♥	♥	♥	♥	♥	♥
Gemini ♊	♥	♥	♥	♥	♥	♥
Cancer ♋	♥	♥	♥	♥	♥	♥
Leo ♌	♥	♥	♥	♥	♥	♥
Virgo ♍	♥	♥	♥	♥	♥	♥
Libra ♎	♥	♥	♥	♥	♥	♥
Scorpio ♏	♥	♥	♥	♥	♥	♥
Sagittarius ♐	♥	♥	♥	♥	♥	♥
Capricorn ♑	♥	♥	♥	♥	♥	♥
Aquarius ♒	♥	♥	♥	♥	♥	♥
Pisces ♓	♥	♥	♥	♥	♥	♥

a :	Scorpio ♏	Sagittarius ♐	Capricorn ♑	Aquarius ♒	Pisces ♓
	♥	♥	♥	♥	♥
	♥	♥	♥	♥	♥
	♥	♥	♥	♥	♥
	♥	♥	♥	♥	♥
	♥	♥	♥	♥	♥
	♥	♥	♥	♥	♥
	♥	♥	♥	♥	♥
	♥	♥	♥	♥	♥
	♥	♥	♥	♥	♥
	♥	♥	♥	♥	♥
	♥	♥	♥	♥	♥

OMG soulmates!

Matching energies.

Totally in sync.

Opposites attract.

Different energies.

It's a struggle.

Not for me.

Never Tell a Sign...

There are just some things better left unsaid!
What little phrase would drive your sign up a wall?
Disclaimer: We're totally not responsible if you use
these to infuriate your friends and family!

Check your Sun and Rising signs.

Never tell...

... an **Aries** they can't do something.

... a **Taurus** the plans have changed.

... a **Gemini** to stop laughing at inappropriate times.

... a **Cancer** that they're a crybaby.

... a **Leo** that you forgot they were even there.

... a **Virgo** to just wing it.

... a **Libra** to make up their minds.

... a **Scorpio** you accidentally spilled their secret.

... a **Sagittarius** to sugarcoat the truth.

... a **Capricorn** to lower their standards.

... an **Aquarius** there's only one way to do something.

... a **Pisces** to give up their alone time.

Late Night Thoughts

It's 1 a.m. and the signs are tossing and turning. What's running through your mind?

Check your Sun and Moon signs.

Aries:

"Okay, maybe I was being petty before, but I still know I was right!"

Taurus:

"Screw it, I'm definitely buying that!"

Gemini:

"This is stupid; why do people even need to sleep?"

Leo:

"Maybe I should redo my entire wardrobe tomorrow!"

Cancer:

"What if all the people I love don't love me back!?"

Virgo:

"Is there a more efficient way to fit sleep into my schedule?"

Capricorn:

"Did I use every waking moment to get my projects done today?"

Aquarius:

"At what elevation does the sky begin?"

Pisces:

"Damn, did I forget to cry today?"

Astrological Love Cats

Let's get romantic! In this special section, we're looking at just what makes each sign swoon and what makes them cringe. Just like with compatibility, we're asking you to take a look at your Venus sign. Venus rules all things love and beauty, so that's where you should look when talking attraction and romance!

Check your Venus, Sun, and Moon.

Aries

"The Thrill-Seeker"
Drawn to: Honesty, spontaneity,
and self-sufficiency

Dislikes: Evasiveness, jealousy,
and lack of humor

Taurus

"The Sensualist"
Drawn to: Reliability, classiness,
and creature comforts

Dislikes: Bad manners, aggression,
and unpredictability

Gemini

"The Partner in Crime"
Drawn to: Wittiness, variety,
and good conversation

Dislikes: Attention hogs, gloomy
people, and dullness

Cancer

"The Protector"
Drawn to: Sentimentality, romantic
gestures, and affection

Dislikes: Arrogance, insensitive
remarks, and aloofness

Leo

"The Romanticist"
Drawn to: Authenticity, loyalty,
and compliments

Dislikes: Straying eyes, negativity,
and patronizing behavior

Virgo

"The Aficionado"
Drawn to: Thoughtfulness,
competence, and personal space

Dislikes: Braggers, tacky things,
and ignorance

Libra

"The Idealist"
Drawn to: Fairness, sharing,
and beautiful things

Dislikes: Exploiters, tactless
people, and confrontation

Scorpio

"The Ride-or-Die"
Drawn to: Boldness, emotional
depth, and devotion

Dislikes: Mediocrity, dishonesty,
and flightiness

Sagittarius

"The Adventurer"

Drawn to: Big ideas, excitement, and free spirits

Dislikes: Being stifled, pessimists, and clinginess

Capricorn

"The Constant Companion"

Drawn to: Ambition, cleverness, and composure

Dislikes: Irresponsibility, inconsistency, and aimlessness

Aquarius

"The Bestie"

Drawn to: Originality, freedom, and intellect

Dislikes: Possessiveness, emotional displays, and rigidity

Pisces

"The Mind-Reader"

Drawn to: Compassion, poetry, and imagination

Dislikes: Detachment, close-mindedness, and rudeness

Element Vibes

Remember back in Astrology 101 when we talked about the elements and signs? Well, you likely share some serious vibes with your elemental comrades! Here are some observations about each elemental group of signs to help you get more in touch with your zodiac.

Check your Sun, Moon, and Rising signs.

Fire
Aries, Leo, Sagittarius

- Either loves you or doesn't care about you at all
- Too lit to quit!
- Allergic to planning things out
- Major chaotic energy
- Will never admit that they need a hug

Earth
Taurus, Virgo, Capricorn

- Total goddess energy
- Worried all the time!
- Gets deeply attached to material objects
- Secretly very sensitive
- Don't even try to pry a secret out of them

Air
Gemini, Libra, Aquarius

- Replies either instantly . . . or two weeks later
- Good-time energy
- Has an opinion on *everything*
- Can roast folks like no other
- Suddenly feels out of place in a crowd

Water
Cancer, Scorpio, Pisces

- Wallowing in a sad playlist
- Can detect BS from a mile away
- Somehow shy, but also not shy at all
- Cries about something that happened in a dream
- Knows everyone's secrets, and keeps 'em

Not-So-Guilty Pleasures

We all indulge in something every once in a while. And is it really a "guilty" pleasure if you're staying in your lane and just enjoying yourself?

Check your Sun, Moon, and Rising signs.

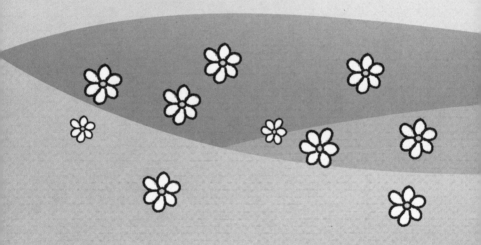

Fire
Aries, Leo, Sagittarius

- A joyride with the music blasting
- Totally unplanned events with tons of surprises
- Taking risks for the adrenaline
- Bragging about liking things before they were cool

Earth
Taurus, Virgo, Capricorn

- A dream date night going exactly to plan
- A luxury spa day, no expense spared!
- Hearing those magical words: "you were right"
- Living their best takeout life

Air
Gemini, Libra, Aquarius

- Ignoring all your texts
- A good TV binge to distract from your overactive mind
- Dipping a toe in each and every trend
- Innocent gossip sessions

Water
Cancer, Scorpio, Pisces

- Turning on your emo playlist for a good wallow
- A secret stash of risqué lingerie
- Weird hobbies no one would ever guess
- Online rabbit holes to escape reality

Chapter 3

Magic

Feeling a little more confident in your astrology skills yet? We know you got this! Now that we've tackled some of the more sensible, earthly stuff, it's time to move on to the magical. Astrology has always been closely related to other divination practices. Many people place it firmly in the category of "witchy stuff," and hey, that's not wrong! Looking up at the stars, charting your past and your future? That's some powerful sorcery.

Magic isn't only spells and crystals, though. Modern witchcraft is made up of an incredibly wide spectrum of practices. Spiritual journeys of all kinds are a sort of witchcraft, whether the seeker realizes it or not. Encountering synchronicities and repeated patterns in your life? Practicing some self-care rituals? Keeping a reflection journal? That's all magic, just like maintaining an altar or casting a spell. Magic is really the result of intention and action. And you can include astrology in taking real, tangible steps along your spiritual journey. In this section, we'll get a little more abstract with the zodiac, touching on everything from tarot to witches to self-care.

Don't let these suggestions limit you, though! We tell y'all which to check as a guide when you're new to astrology. The more you learn, the more easily you'll be able to apply the ideas to your other placements. Always do what feels right.

> Again, we recommend checking certain signs for each section. You always check your Sun sign, because that is your core personality. You'd check your Moon sign when a section has more focus on your feelings, your fears, or your needs. And your Rising sign? Check that when we're talking about interactions, opinions, or your skills.

Tarot and the Signs

Did you know that each astrology sign has an associated Major Arcana tarot card? Tarot cards, like astrology, have been used for both divination and self-examination for hundreds of years.

The most popular tarot deck is the Rider-Waite version, with some beautiful, archetype-heavy illustrations by Pamela Coleman Smith. The following meanings, zodiac associations, and tarot cards are influenced by the Rider-Waite tarot deck. Find your card!

Check your Sun and Moon signs.

Aries: The Emperor

THE EMPEROR

The Emperor symbolizes a powerful figure, positively brimming with authority and self-assurance. The Emperor is perched upon a throne carved with rams, so it should come as no surprise that Aries is connected to these powerful, bad babe vibes! Confidence? Check. Natural leader? Check. Loyalty through the roof? Check! Like an Aries, The Emperor is big on honesty, straightforwardness, and being their best self. Both sign and card are typically more benevolent than malicious, with no time for mind games.

When you see this card, you know it's time to flex your power. Channel that ready-to-take-on-the-world energy, Aries!

Taurus: The Hierophant

When you want something done diligently, you go to a Taurus. Their tarot card is The Hierophant, also known as the high priest. This card encourages you to learn from tried-and-true methods, examining traditions and conventions to find wisdom. The Hierophant, like Taurus, is not afraid of hard work, knowing that achieving truly great things takes serious dedication. There's no rushing wisdom, and there's no rushing a Taurus. The Hierophant has secured an enviable position in life, which takes slow and steady perseverance. Plus, the perks of being on top aren't bad!

THE HIEROPHANT

When you see this card, ask yourself whether you're putting in the time and energy needed to reach your goals. And perhaps more importantly, are you enjoying the successes you have earned? A Taurus works hard, but should also play hard!

THE LOVERS

Gemini: The Lovers

As a dual sign, Gemini is clearly associated with The Lovers card! The couple depicted in The Lovers represents variety, duality, and seeing things from other people's perspectives. Geminis love keeping their options open, and The Lovers card smiles on those who consider things from all angles. What ideas or concepts do you place the greatest value upon? How do you reconcile all kinds of diverse energies into a beautiful whole?

When you see this card, think harmony. It's a reminder that no matter how out of whack you're feeling, you can find your way to a workable balance. Geminis can deftly juggle many different personas, striking an equilibrium where others might be lost.

Cancer: The Chariot

Cancer gets cast as the emotional one, like, a lot. The thing is, most people overlook the fact that Cancer is the cardinal water sign. They're courageous and aren't afraid to jump into action, so it makes sense that Cancer is represented by The Chariot. Cancers might come at a situation a little crab-like, but you can bet they'll be coming regardless! The Chariot depicts a warrior rushing toward victory, overcoming any and all obstacles on their path. Cancers tend to get what they want, after all!

THE CHARIOT

When you see this card, it's a sign to take charge. Good things come to those who go after what they want. Comfort zones might be, well, comfortable, but you have to chase your dreams!

Leo: Strength

Bold Leo is associated with the Strength tarot card. Yeah, this one is pretty obvious, with the lion right there on the card, huh? But a little less apparent is the compassion represented by this card. It's not just bravery, confidence, and daring on display here, though Leos do have all those qualities in spades. There's a sense of strength of character, of generosity of spirit. Leos are among the most bighearted of the zodiac, always willing to help a friend in need.

When you see this card, think staying power and exuberance. You have quite the wellspring of fortitude backing you up. Never forget who you are! Radiate that Leo confidence!

Virgo: The Hermit

When you think about Virgo's calling to purify and perfect, it's not hard to see why they're connected to The Hermit. Virgo is driven by a desire to cleanse away the old and obsolete to make room for the new. The Hermit is right here with them. This card is big on seeking a deeper understanding and looking inward. Like Virgo, The Hermit asks you to reexamine the way you've been doing things. What no longer serves you? What do you want to take with you into your next phase of life?

When you see this card, it's a call to examine your inner discipline. Virgos are known for being hardworking perfectionists. While it's all well and good to want to do things right, just make sure you're not being too much of a stickler! Completing your goal at a high standard is always better than never finishing it in pursuit of utter, unattainable perfection.

Libra: Justice

Symbolized by the scales, Libra is connected to the Justice card. Libra is all about balance, harmony, and symmetry. Libras are famous for their indecisiveness, but that's more a result of their desire to see everything from every possible perspective. Symmetry, remember? It's very Libra, and very Justice, to take every opinion out there, weigh them all, and deliver a compromise they deem fair.

When you see this card, remember that what goes around comes around. Maintain a sense of balance and integrity in your dealings, Libra style. You know what's right.

Scorpio: Death

Scorpios have quite the reputation, just like the Death tarot card. In both cases, there's more going on than meets the eye, and both can easily be misunderstood. Yes, Scorpio has an undeniable, potent magnetism. Yes, Death depicts a skeleton riding a horse, a grim reaper arriving in the aftermath of a battle. Both are pretty dang intense. But both sign and card find their power in transformation, in changes as a result of struggle. Scorpio and Death are both about growth and metamorphosis. Change is rarely easy, but it is necessary for new life.

When you see this card, don't freak out! Channel that Scorpio ability to look darkness and trauma in the eye, knowing you will rise again. You might be different, but you will be stronger.

Sagittarius: Temperance

Always seeking some higher truth, Sagittarius is the philosopher of the zodiac, a doer with their eyes on the horizon. Temperance is the card linked to Sagittarius. This card is graced with a peaceful, angelic being, pouring truth from one cup to another. Temperance is depicted with one foot on the Earth, representing the need to stay grounded, while the other dips into the waters of the spiritual realm. That divine guidance, received here on Earth? Does that sound a little like enlightenment? Because that's pretty much the Sagittarius dream. Why else are they always looking to learn more, see more, and understand more?

When you see this card, check back in with your roots. You might be reaching for some lofty ideal, which is admirable! Make sure one of those feet stays grounded, though. Everything in moderation.

Capricorn: The Devil

The Devil is another of those commonly misunderstood tarot cards, which makes it all the more appropriate that it's associated with the oft-misunderstood Capricorn. This card symbolizes desire, vices, and power dynamics. Capricorns might come across as rather stoic or serious to some, but you'd be hard-pressed to find someone more driven to achieve their ambitions. The Devil, ruler of their domain, certainly doesn't think small, and neither does Capricorn. The vice part? Well, Capricorns are known to both work hard and play hard. They can go way too hard in either direction here, falling into either a dangerous workaholic mode or overindulging in life's luxuries. Don't be your own worst enemy!

When you see this card, take a look at your values and your goals. Are they in alignment? It's also a little reminder that it's okay to pamper yourself once in a while!

Aquarius: The Star

It's always a breath of fresh air when The Star comes up in a reading. It's a symbol of hope and possibilities. This is the kind of vibe that Aquarius gives when they get involved with just about anything. Aquarius folks are positively bursting at the seams with innovations and creative solutions, and more than that, they know the value of taking real action. They're not ones to wallow in despair, instead choosing to believe in their ability to make a better future. And just look at that card! You can't get more "water bearer" than someone pouring forth water they've been carrying.

When you see this card, it's a message that even when times look dark, there's a star there to guide you back home. Spoiler alert: You are that star! You always have the ability to love yourself, and the skills to better your life.

Pisces: The Moon

Dreamy, intuitive Pisces and The Moon card go hand in hand. The Moon symbolizes the subconscious, dreams, and illusions. Things aren't always as they seem when The Moon comes up in a reading, and Pisces understands that on an instinctive level. While these watery souls can be easily swept up in dreamworlds and are prone to falling under the spell of manipulators, they can also sense when something feels off. Pisces are a lot stronger than many people realize. They can walk that path toward the unknown, on the narrow line between the tame and the wild.

THE MOON

When you see this card, take some time to reflect. Your intuition will never steer you wrong, and The Moon encourages you to trust in yourself. Shake off the illusions and see what's really going on!

Oracle Cards for the Signs

Oracle cards are an amazing self-reflection tool that can help guide you in the right direction. While oracle card meanings are a bit more free-flowing and intuitive than tarot cards, they're still an awesome way to get to the heart of things.

We've drawn two Pulp Oracle cards for each sign. Be open-minded when you see your card! Does one speak more strongly to your Sun? Which one hits that tender spot inside for your Moon? For your Rising, reflect on your current social circle or work life. Let go of any expectations and see how the imagery and interpretations relate to you.

Check your Sun, Moon, and Rising signs.

Aries

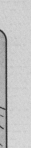

The Lighter

- Seeing hope on the horizon
- Starting something new
- Boosted sense of passion and health
- Beware of burnout

The Fern

- Feeling restless or in need of a creative outlet
- Discarding baseless fears to uncover the truth
- Success in an upcoming project
- Beware of neglecting your health

Taurus

The Crescent Moon

- Taking steps toward achieving a goal
- Portent of creative bursts ahead
- Feeling optimistic about the future
- Beware of being complacent

The Pumpkin

- Actualizing abundance and well-being
- Seeing the fruits of your labor
- Enjoying the present moment
- Beware of overspending

Gemini

The Lava Lamp

- Enjoying the strange and unusual
- Stepping out of your comfort zone
- Slowing down once in a while
- Beware of pushing things too far

The Clam Shell

- Building strong connections with other people
- Getting involved with the world
- An omen of wealth and abundance
- Beware of clamming up and keeping secrets

Cancer

The Houseplant

- Enjoying slow but steady progress
- Realizing the full potential of hard work
- Healing from a physical or emotional hurt
- Beware of trying to control everything

The Flannel Shirt

- Period of warmth and happiness
- Sense of relief regarding a situation
- Feeling protected and welcome
- Beware of complacency

Leo

The Crystal

- Feeling in perfect unity with your path
- Doing the work to heal from past trauma
- Seizing the opportunities that come to you
- Beware of ignoring your natural gifts

The Magic Potion

- Power to alter a situation
- Using financial success wisely
- Taking responsibility for actions
- Beware of risky shortcuts

Virgo

The Mushroom

- Portent of a financial windfall
- Growing through any struggle
- Feeling a desire to escape
- Beware of mental exhaustion

The Cauldron

- Reclaiming control of your life
- Selflessness and helping others
- Trusting your emotional perceptions
- Beware of rigidity

Libra

The Daisy

- Upcoming period of good luck
- New beginnings or renewed bonds
- Feeling called to transform
- Beware of indecisiveness

The Mirror

- Self-reflection and a feeling of wholeness
- Emotions surfacing from the subconscious
- Facing a challenge with inner strength
- Beware of forming a bad habit

Scorpio

The Dried Flowers

- Connection to the past
- Trusting your instincts
- Pursuing some inner desire
- Beware of getting stuck in your head

The Open Eye

- Foreshadowing important decisions to come
- Delving into your subconscious
- Challenge to expand your horizons
- Beware of rigid worldviews

Sagittarius

The Butterfly

- Pursuing something or someone new
- A time of transformation is upon you
- Leveled-up awareness
- Beware of feeling out of the loop

The Spiral

- Moving forward on the spiritual journey
- Recognizing lessons that need to be learned
- Letting go in order to grow
- Beware of obsession

Capricorn

The Candle Lantern

- Finding a light in the dark
- Small things growing bigger and better
- Searching the subconscious for truth
- Beware of ignoring a problem

The Squirrel

- Period of abundance
- Laying a stable foundation
- Work hard, play hard
- Beware of forgetting something important

Aquarius

The Black Cat

- Sense of mystery and restlessness
- Recognizing a message from the universe
- Allowing yourself to be more spontaneous
- Beware of compromising your principles

The Oyster's Pearl

- Portent of amazing news
- Serenity and reflection
- Wisdom gained from experience
- Beware of shutting others out

Pisces

The Record Player

- Listening and expanding your horizons
- Tapping into creative abilities
- Navigating a difficult situation with grace
- Beware of hiding from your mistakes

The Frog

- Transitioning from the old to the n
- Cleansing the air in a situation or relationship
- Finding a better future after emotional hurt
- Beware of hiding your true feelings

Self-care for the Mind, Body, and Soul: Astrology Style

Life has its ups and downs, darling, no matter what your zodiac sign is. We all deal with stress and anxiety in different ways. Keep reading for some sign-specific affirmations for your mind, some tangible actions for your body, and some reflections for your soul. You might feel more connected to the BODY actions for your Sun, while vibing a bit more with your Moon sign for the MIND and SOUL. Allow yourself to be flexible!

Check your Sun and Moon signs.

Aries

Mind

- My soul is radiant, and I nourish it with love.
- I surrender and allow my desires to flow to me.
- I believe in my ability to truly love myself for who I am.

Body

- Think about one thing you're dying to do. Take a step toward it.
- Get in touch with your inner child and frolic in a sunny field.
- Stretch and melt your stress away on the yoga mat.

Soul

- What is really worth your fiery energy?
- I am fierce AF, and I've got this!
- It's totally cool to make a big deal about the things I love.

Taurus

Mind

- I accept my emotions even when I don't understand them.
- I am building a life of happiness and success.
- The more I let go, the better I will feel.

Body

- Take a little road trip with a friend, change your surroundings up.
- Close your eyes, turn your mind off, and just breathe deeply for a few minutes.
- Pay attention to how your daily routine makes you feel. Is it bringing comfort or stress?

Soul

- Be forgiving.
- Tidy my mind. Align myself. I got this.
- I let go of expectations and open up to what I need.

Gemini

Mind

- I am becoming the best version of myself.
- Every new step takes me on a fulfilling, exciting, and wild ride!
- I am strong enough to be myself.

Body

- Go on a date with yourself. You deserve to be pampered!
- Open a window and breathe in some fresh air.
- Put in some friend time. Make plans with or chat up your besties.

Soul

- My purpose is too great to quit. I will see it through.
- Are you being mindful about the reality you're creating?
- Pretending not to care is not the same as letting go.

Cancer

Mind

- I'm cute as heck and only accept the best.
- I'm in alignment with my dreams.
- My inner peace cannot be disturbed.

Body

- Cuddle up with a good book and escape reality for a bit.
- Spend some precious time with your fur baby.
- Journal those feelings out. It helps sometimes just to spill.

Soul

- I receive what I put into the world.
- I acknowledge and respect my limits.
- I speak to myself with kindness always.

Leo

Mind

- I let go of what I outgrow.
- I will not dim my radiance for anyone or anything.
- Every decision I make is the right one for me.

Body

- Dance around to a nostalgic song.
- Treat yourself. Plan a massage, pampering sesh, or even just a nice hot soak in the tub.
- Take yourself out to the movies.

Soul

- I will stop worrying about things I cannot control.
- I break free from the past.
- I prioritize my love for myself over being loved by others.

Virgo

Mind

- I am forgiving of myself and everyone else.
- I release all blockages and transmute all my pain into growth and love.
- I'm ready to let go. I'm ready for what's next.

Body

- Clean up your space and reorganize a cluttered area.
- Make a gratitude list of all the things that bring you joy daily.
- Listen to some chill music and cozy up on the couch.

Soul

- My path is not a straight line; it's a spiral. As I come back around, I recognize the deeper truths.
- Thoughts aren't facts. Don't believe everything you think.
- Have no fear! Trust yourself and trust the universe.

Libra

Mind

- I listen to my intuition and trust my inner guide.
- My energy is radiant, even in the midst of chaos.
- I give myself permission to do what is right for me.

Body

- Burn some incense and cleanse the energy of your space.
- Buy yourself a beautiful bouquet and enjoy nature's colors.
- Put on your favorite outfit and take some selfies, you fabulous babe!

Soul

- I will focus on progress rather than perfection. I've come so far.
- I set, honor, and respect my own boundaries.
- I will stop saying sorry for showing my emotions.

Scorpio

Mind

- It's okay for me to say "no" for my mental health.
- I have amazing ideas and my voice deserves to be heard.
- I consciously create my future.

Body

- Go to a place where you feel at peace and practice meditating.
- Find a new blend of soothing tea and let the warm vibes help you unwind.
- Get creative and work on a crafty project.

Soul

- I will talk to myself a little nicer today.
- No one needs to believe in me but me.
- The best is yet to come; stay focused.

Sagittarius

Mind

- I lead a life of excitement and purpose.
- The universe has big plans for me, and I'm open and ready to embrace them.
- I have the strength to overcome anything.

Body

- Make a mood playlist related to how you're feeling right now.
- Practice some self-love affirmations in the mirror.
- Go outside and soak in some sun rays.

Soul

- I love who I am right now.
- What I think, I become; what I feel, I attract.
- What is coming is better than what is gone.

Capricorn

Mind

- I am endlessly creating myself.
- I relax and let go; my life is in perfect flow.
- I put my energy into things that matter to me.

Body

- Put down your phone for a night and take a social media break.
- Go outside and wander freely for a while to clear your head.
- Watch a funny movie or show—laughter helps!

Soul

- I don't owe anyone an explanation.
- Productivity doesn't define my worth.
- I'm proud of how far I've come, how hard I work, and how much I care.

Aquarius

Mind

- Life treats me well and I treat myself well.
- I let go of all beliefs that have been holding me back.
- I breathe in relaxation and breathe out tension.

Body

- Practice breathwork.
- Give yourself a tarot reading.
- Find a workshop to learn more about something you have a passion for.

Soul

- It's okay to not know what's next and to let go of expectations.
- When things change inside me, things change around me.
- Time heals almost everything. I will be patient with myself.

Pisces

Mind

- I become more and more calm with every breath I take.
- I am right where I am supposed to be.
- My intuition guides me and keeps me on the right path.

Body

- Start a new journal, and let your thoughts freely flow as you write.
- Listen to a random playlist and discover new music.
- Clean out any clutter from your space and start fresh.

Soul

- Empathy without boundaries is self-destruction.
- Every next level of my life will require a different me.
- I will trust the timing of the universe, it has my back.

What You Need When Stressed Out

You deserve some downtime! Sometimes figuring out what helps you relax takes a little practice. Try some of these tips based on your elemental type.

Check your Sun and Moon signs.

Fire

Aries, Leo, Sagittarius

- Get a healthy dose of fresh air.
- Rewatch your favorite movie.
- Make an impromptu dance party.
- Change your scenery.
- Make a mood board for a future adventure.
- Turn off your mind and take a nap.

Earth

Taurus, Virgo, Capricorn

- Take a hot bubble bath with a glass of wine.
- Speed clean your space.
- Check things off a to-do list.
- Try the perfect aromatherapy blend.
- Order in and marathon your fave show.
- Add ten minutes of mindfulness to your routine.

Air

Gemini, Libra, Aquarius

- Journal your thoughts out.
- Find someone to talk it all out with.
- Treat yourself to something special.
- Plan a game night with friends.
- Pretend it's the '90s and stay off social media for a night.
- Find a new dance tutorial online.

Water

Cancer, Scorpio, Pisces

- Find some time to escape it all.
- Retreat into your comfort zone.
- Take a break from social media.
- Create a nostalgic playlist.
- Cultivate and visit your personal safe space daily.
- Let your emotions flow through you until the wave passes.

Grounding Exercises

Feeling overwhelmed? Engulfed by all the demands on your time? Maybe you're dealing with an emotionally demanding situation. Babe, you got to take care of you first! What good decisions are made from a place of chaos and confusion? Yeah, not too many. It's important to create a safe place from which to approach your problem. That's where grounding techniques come in.

Grounding exercises are a phenomenal way of bringing that turmoil under control. It allows you to gain a measure of control over your feelings and reactions, like hitting pause until you're calmer and better equipped to find solutions. Like any new exercise, it may take some practice to find what works for you, but ultimately, being able to bring yourself a sense of peace is 100 percent worth it.

Here are some element-specific grounding exercises to try. Find a comfy, quiet space and take some time to get and stay grounded. Remember, this is a practice; you will improve your skills with regular repetition. It might feel weird at first, but keep at it. There's real science behind these techniques.

Check your Sun and Moon signs.

Fire

Aries, Leo, Sagittarius

These action-orientated signs would benefit from physically checking in on themselves. When you're feeling tense, you can reach—and maintain—a state of relaxation by incorporating the following body-scanning exercise.

1. Find a comfortable spot to lie down. Take a few deep breaths, into and out of the belly.
2. Bring your awareness to your feet. Observe the sensations, and maintain that deep belly breathing.
3. Slowly, move your awareness up through your feet, to your ankles, your legs, your hips, all the way on up to the crown of your head.
4. Intentionally notice how each body part feels as you move up. If you're feeling particularly tense in one area, it's okay to linger there for a while, breathing into the sensation. Visualize your muscles loosening as you exhale stress and tension and inhale peace and love.
5. Scan up and down as much as needed. Notice how you feel now as opposed to when you first started. Repeat whenever you need some grounding.

Earth

Taurus, Virgo, Capricorn

Earth signs are typically pretty grounded, but they have a tendency to get wrapped up in their own heads, feeding into an ever-deepening spiral of anxiety and overthinking. Check back in with your senses and get out of your head using this technique.

1. Take some deep breaths, focusing on pushing air out of your nose, then breathing deeply into your belly.
2. Shift your focus to a favorite item of yours, or even just an object within reach.
3. Touch the object and feel its shape, texture, and temperature with your fingers. Find the nooks and crannies that feel good in your hands.
4. Bring your other senses into focus. Notice the familiar scent, the sound of your fingers brushing across the object. Observe the colors and markings. If it's an edible object, like a fruit or cookie, taste it. Let it play across your tongue.
5. Repeat this exercise as often as needed. You are here, right now.

Air

Gemini, Libra, Aquarius

With so much energy spent on communication and big ideas, air signs have a penchant for racing thoughts. Sometimes it can feel like you're trapped under an avalanche of ideas. When the big picture is feeling too heavy, try this grounding technique to shrink the world down to size.

1. Find a detailed photograph or image. This can be your own image, or something you found online.
2. Take in the details for fifteen to twenty seconds. Notice what's in the frame, and what the context may be outside it. What's the subject of the image? What colors drew you to it?
3. Look away from the photograph and recreate it in your mind. Start from the most vivid detail you remember and build outward. It doesn't need to be perfect!
4. Now that you've focused on building that image, make a mental list of all the things you can remember. Call to mind the colors, the people, the context, and so on.
5. Repeat whenever you're confronted by thoughts that feel like they're moving 100 miles per hour. Bonus: You'll also be sharpening your memory!

Water

Cancer, Scorpio, Pisces

Highly intuitive water signs are easily swept up in emotions, borne along on both their own turbulent feelings and other people's pain. Your natural empathy can be both a blessing and a curse sometimes. It's important to create a place of safety you can retreat to. When you can't do so literally, try this visualization grounding technique.

1. Find a comfortable spot and close your eyes. Choose a position that's comfortable for you. Some people like sitting cross-legged, while others like to lie flat on their backs. Breathe deeply through the nose.
2. Visualize a door opening onto a cozy, calm space. As you step through the door, breathe out. Let your tension and worry slip out with that exhale.
3. In this space, you are calm and safe. Mentally fill your visualization with your favorite comforts. Paint the walls your favorite shade, fall back into a relaxing pile of squishy, soft pillows. Reach out to touch your pet. Run your fingers across your favorite books or the leaves of your plants.
4. Enjoy some time in this personal safe space. Wrap yourself in a cozy blanket and allow your breathing to soften into a natural, calm rhythm.
5. Return to your safe haven whenever you need to. You can change up the scenery whenever you want. This is *your* personal sanctuary.

Lucky Amulets

Who couldn't use a little extra dose of luck? We've gathered both a lucky amulet and a crystal for each sign. Boost your own luck by finding a way to carry one of these on you whenever needed. Disclaimer: Scorpios, please only carry your own skull around. Jewelry is okay!

Aries

cacti and carnelian

Taurus

ladybug and rose quartz

Gemini

butterfly and citrine quartz

Cancer

seashells and moonstone

Leo

acorn and tiger's eye

Virgo

bamboo and selenite

Libra

rainbow and lapis lazuli

Scorpio

skull and obsidian

Sagittarius

dice and smoky quartz

Capricorn

lucky coin and jade

Aquarius

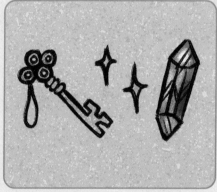

key and amethyst

Pisces

goldfish and chrysocolla

What Type of Witch Are You?

We all have a little bit (or maybe a lot) of magic in us! When you get in touch with your witchy side, you'll find that you may be drawn to certain elements. There are a lot of witchcraft styles out there. Which one resonates with your astrological flavor? You might blend these techniques in your own life if you practice. You have your whole chart making you, you, after all! We've been doing a lot of elemental and modality grouping for signs, but we're switching it up a bit here. We matched two signs with each type of witch based on some key similarities they share.

Check your Sun and Moon signs.

Cosmic Witch: Aries and Gemini

- Harnesses power of the planets and the cosmos
- Decorates with star charts, sunny tones, and amethyst crystals
- Thrives on high-paced energy
- Recharges vibes by spending time under the stars

Green Witch: Taurus and Sagittarius

- Draws power from nature and living things
- Decorates with lots of plants, jewel tones, and prehnite crystals
- Feels happiest after spending time in nature
- Recharges vibes by pressing flowers or tending to plants

Kitchen Witch: Cancer and Leo

- Works with food and drink to cast their spells
- Decorates with herbs, earthy tones, and carnelian crystals
- Makes food to nourish their loved ones
- Recharges vibes with candles and food

Healing Witch: Virgo and Libra

- Loves working with crystals and energy
- Decorates with crystals, light blue tones, and clear quartz
- Feels most fulfilled when helping others
- Recharges vibes by cleansing crystals for balancing chakras

Sea Witch: Scorpio and Capricorn

- Has a strong connection to the power of the sea
- Decorates with shells, blue tones, and aquamarine crystals
- Has a deep affinity for storms
- Recharges vibes by being in water

Divination Witch: Aquarius and Pisces

- Naturally drawn to practices like tarot and runes
- Decorates with crystal balls, purple tones, and azurite crystals
- Has serious psychic energy
- Recharges vibes by consulting tarot cards

Chapter 4

Just for Fun

You've come quite a way on your Pulp Astrology journey, from acing a crash course on your personal planets to picking up some practical magic. We're proud of you! You've put in the work; now it's time for a little play.

The next sections are all about food, fun, and playing dress-up. How in the world does that relate to astrology, you may ask? Perhaps you've never wondered what your vampire persona would be like, or what takeout food is your sign's spiritual counterpart. That's totally fine, because we have! Going forward, let your imagination run wild. Remember when we said immersing yourself in the material is the best way to learn? You now have all the tools you need to understand just how each sign ticks. So let loose and have some fun!

Plus, you're probably getting to be quite a pro at talking astrology. Feel free to look at your other placements to get a feel for your own chart as a whole. You're the best person to understand all your own complexities!

For the next sections, we continue to give you specific placements to check. By now, we're sure you know to always check your Sun sign because it's your central self. Your Moon sign has more influence on emotional well-being and needs, while your Rising sign comes into play when others interact with you, and you with them.

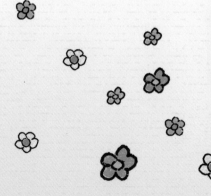

Mixology for the Signs

You're a perfectly blended cocktail of your entire birth chart, balanced together ever so carefully. In case you've ever wondered how to mix up the quintessential Aquarius or the most potent Scorpio, we've drawn up the tried-and-true recipe cards for each sign right here. We recommend spicing up the recipe with a dash from your Moon and Rising signs, but don't make it too overpowering!

Check your Sun, Moon, and Rising signs.

Aries

Ingredients

- 2 shots of excitement
- 1 part optimism
- A dash of impatience

Instructions

- Stir and garnish with lots of laughs.

Taurus

Ingredients

- 2 oz aesthetics
- 1 oz treating yourself
- A pinch of guilty pleasures

Instructions

- Shake all the ingredients together and dust with juicy gossip.

Gemini

Ingredients

- 2 parts high energy
- 1½ parts hilarious
- A pinch of moodiness

Instructions

- Mix well and top with charisma.

Cancer

Ingredients

- 3 oz compassion
- 1 tsp of nostalgia
- A pinch of tears

Instructions

- Blend well and sprinkle with loyalty.

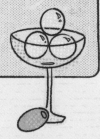

Leo

Ingredients

- 2½ shots of passion
- 1 part generosity
- A pinch of drama

Instructions

- Shake and garnish with glamour.

Virgo

Ingredients

- 2 parts multitasking
- 1½ parts intelligence
- A bit of overthinking it

Instructions

- Mix together and add some kindness.

Libra

Ingredients

- 2 parts pure charm
- 1 part looking cute
- A hint of indecision

Instructions

- Shake vigorously and decorate with romance.

Scorpio

Ingredients

- 2 oz determination
- 1 oz fierceness
- A smidge of secrets

Instructions

- Stir together and dust with intuition.

Sagittarius

Ingredients

- 3 shots of comedic timing
- 1 oz of freedom
- A sprinkle of sass

Instructions

- Blend well and top with curiosity.

Capricorn

Ingredients

- 2 oz class
- 1½ oz ambition
- 1 tsp of sarcasm

Instructions

- Pour together the ingredients and finish with self-control.

Aquarius

Ingredients

- 3 parts originality
- 1 part humanitarianism
- A pinch of skepticism

Instructions

- Mix up the ingredients and garnish with independence.

Pisces

Ingredients

- 2 shots of empathy
- 1½ shots of imagination
- ½ oz hiding from problems

Instructions

- Shake all of the ingredients and add a dash of selflessness.

Your Magic Ingredient

Now that you know the essential components of your lovely zodiac cocktail, let's conjure up a little bit of magic! What little touch really ties everything together for your placements? Be proud of the magic you're bringing to the table.

Check your Sun, Moon, and Rising signs.

ARIES: A large dash of raw energy.

TAURUS: A healthy dash of decadence.

GEMINI: A pinch of natural charisma.

CANCER: A bunch of compassion for others.

LEO: A pinch of being just a bit extra.

VIRGO: A hint of my way or the highway.

LIBRA: One part being an amazing friend.

SCORPIO: Two parts overwhelming emotion.

SAGITTARIUS: A hearty dose of adventure.

CAPRICORN: A bunch of the finer things in life.

AQUARIUS: A hearty dose of personal freedom.

PISCES: A dash of avoiding conflict.

The Signs as Movie Genres

It's movie night! Let's pretend we're back in the days of the video store, when you had to pick just one movie and hope to heck it was good when you got it home. With your entire night on the line, what genre do you make a beeline toward?

It shouldn't surprise you that your zodiac sign has an influence on your entertainment tastes. Some people just can't resist the heartbreaking sob story—we're looking at you, water signs—and others need a lot more action to keep them engaged. Find your next favorite film by trusting in your astrology sign!

Check your Sun and Moon signs. If you're watching with others, add in the Rising sign.

Aries

1970s Car Chase Flick

Our fast-moving fiery darlings love to get the heart racing and the heat on! Scratch that action-babe itch with a totally iconic 1970s car chase movie. Get that adrenaline going and claim the obscure film–watcher trophy at the same time.

Taurus

Any Aesthetic Film

Good luck getting a Taurus to waste their precious relaxation time on something icky or unattractive. With all that Venus energy driving them, Taurus would be happy watching anything aesthetically pleasing. They want a lovely dreamworld to settle into for a while!

Gemini

Spicy Summer Camp Comedy

Geminis are known for their mercurial ways, quickly jumping from one interest to the next. Drawn-out or dreary movies really rain on their cheerful parade, so they'd do best choosing a fast-moving summer camp laugh fest.

Cancer

Sultry Film Noir

A true hopeless romantic at heart, Cancer lives for the kind of high-stakes drama and raw vulnerability found in an authentic film noir. They'll resonate with the femme fatale lead, because they're secretly one of the fiercest signs in the entire zodiac!

Leo

Mob Boss Crime Drama

Born to be the biggest and baddest personality around, Leos are known for having a taste for the high life. And who lives more decadently than a mob boss? That enviable VIP status? Fancy jewelry? Topped off with a dramatic grand exit? Yes, please!

Virgo

2000s Indie Slice of Life

With their tendency to get wrapped up in their own worries and anxieties, Virgos would do well to unwind with a heartfelt yet chill movie, like a slice of life indie dramedy. Finding a hidden gem of a soundtrack is only an added bonus!

Libra

Impeccably Styled Cult Horror

It may surprise some people, but lovely, graceful Libra is a sucker for a cult horror flick with phenomenal art direction. They do love to watch some drama, and what's a horror movie but a drama turned up to eleven? Plus, they get to brag about their obscure tastes.

Scorpio

Any Cerebral Film

Scorpio craves intensity. Even in their recreational time, they're looking for a film that gets, well, weird. Very comfortable with the uncomfortable, Scorpios would love a super cerebral movie, complete with surreal dream sequences and bizarre plotlines.

Sagittarius

Quirky Whodunit

Ever the celestial truth-seeker, Sagittarius should look for a more lighthearted whodunit comedy. Not only can they puzzle out the mystery along with the characters, but they'll also get to laugh a lot along the way. Relaxing and flexing that brain all at the same time!

Capricorn

Riveting, Eye-opening Documentary

Capricorns have their day usually pretty packed already, so a movie has to be good for them to make time for it. A truly riveting documentary about something they never knew is a great fit for them. Plus, they'll pick up some new useful knowledge along the way!

Aquarius

Close Encounter Sci-Fi Thriller

Aquarius should lean into their reputation for being a bit out there and take in a sci-fi thriller. It's not really about the aliens, anyway; it's about how society responds to big changes. Aquarians will love seeing problems being solved through innovation and collaboration.

Pisces

1980s Fantasy Quest

As the resident dreamer of the zodiac, Pisces prefer their films to transport them to an entirely different world. A 1980s fantasy with a quest to save the world is right up their alley! They'll get all wrapped up in the journey and celebrate right alongside the heroes at the end.

Spring, Summer, Fall, and Winter

What's your sign up to throughout the year? We all handle the seasons a bit differently. If you're an outdoorsy type, you're probably out there rain, snow, or shine. Maybe you simply adore summer . . . through your floor-to-ceiling windows, in an air-conditioned room. What's your sign's take on each of the seasons?

Check your Sun and Rising signs.

Aries

Spring

- Practically climbing the walls to get outside after winter
- Springing impromptu plans on all their friends

Summer

- Heading to the amusement park
- The first one to jump in the pool

Fall

- Looking for the scariest haunted house to visit
- Plays their favorite spooky playlist on repeat

Winter

- Ready for all the winter activities
- Goes stir-crazy being stuck inside on a snow day

Taurus

Spring

- Living their best aesthetic picnic life
- Strategically changing up their wardrobe

Summer

- Setting up a chic yet comfy outdoor movie night
- Perfects their charcuterie board with seasonal selections

Fall

- Low-key their favorite season
- Chunky sweaters galore

Winter

- Fills their home with plants and pretends it's spring
- Treats this season like self-care season

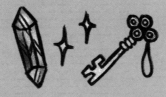

Gemini

Spring

- Getting a jump start on a hot summer
- Planning tons of get-togethers with friends

Summer

- Getting into some crazy mischief
- Camping trip? Hell yeah!

Fall

- Fascinated by the constant changes
- Feels like there's never enough time for all the fall activities

Winter

- Trying—and failing—to learn patience
- Half hibernation mode, half hyperactive mode

Cancer

Spring

- Gets very nostalgic and indulges their inner child
- Plans a beautiful, flowery photoshoot

Summer

- Going all out for a beach bonfire
- Happily enjoying their air conditioning, cuddled up with a great book

Fall

- Pumpkin spice everything!
- Copious amounts of cozy blankets and movie nights

Winter

- Trying out a new recipe daily
- Loves the look of winter, but staying inside

Leo

Spring

- Dressing like it's already summer
- Vibing to an upbeat playlist

Summer

- Living for BBQs and late-night dance parties
- Summer fashion shopping spree!

Fall

- Planning the wildest Halloween looks
- Feeling a bit sad about the cloudy skies and cold weather

Winter

- Rocking faux furs all winter
- Filming all their seasonal makeup looks

Virgo

Spring

- Legit excited for spring cleaning
- Visiting all the cute flea markets and craft fairs

Summer

- Repotting and planting a whole forest of leafy friends
- Learning to identify wildlife on a nature walk

Fall

- Takes a social media break
- Crafting the perfect autumn playlist

Winter

- In disaster prep mode at the first sign of snow
- Reads a million books under a heated blanket

Libra

Spring

- New season, new crushes to stalk
- Sipping on the new iced tea trend all day

Summer

- Stargazing with their loved one
- So excited for all the live music!

Fall

- Hitting the pumpkin patch, apple orchards, and all the parties
- Has all their Halloween decor up on the first day of fall

Winter

- Moisturizing day and night
- Binges trashy reality TV all winter

Scorpio

Spring

- Taking advantage of the people-watching weather
- Going on solo walks around town

Summer

- Going for long drives at night with the windows down
- Catching up on indie movie flicks

Fall

- Roping friends into Ouija sessions and ghost hunts
- Thriving hard on the otherworldly vibes

Winter

- Giving the *best* surprise gifts . . . because they know your secrets
- Stays in bed all day, still looks hot as hell

Sagittarius

Spring
- Ready to make some bad decisions
- Hanging out with friends as much as possible

Summer
- Getting in as many trips in as possible!
- Cracking jokes around the campfire

Fall
- Sucker for all the cutesy Halloween movies
- Planning leaf-peeping road trips

Winter
- Sledding, skating, skiing . . . you name it!
- Trying to stay optimistic all winter

Capricorn

Spring
- Soaking in the fresh air, new life, and latest opportunities
- Excited to try all the new places opening up

Summer
- Finally lets themselves take a vacation
- Then launches another small business

Fall
- Breaks out their impressive outerwear collection
- Already planning their holiday gift buying

Winter
- Secretly on an emotional roller coaster all winter
- Already lining up their spring plans

Aquarius

Spring

- Too busy enjoying life to text back
- Sitting outside at a cute café or park

Summer

- Living for all the outdoor activities
- Revisiting childhood and hitting the arcade

Fall

- Getting ultra-nostalgic and more introspective
- Planning a cozy weekly game night with their besties

Winter

- Low-key loves the cold
- Embracing crazy sleeping patterns

Pisces

Spring

- Switching over to their upbeat playlists
- Feeling lighter and freer than they have in months

Summer

- Soaking up the good vibes at a music festival
- Canoeing, fishing, hiking, swimming . . . you name it!

Fall

- Spending time getting pleasantly lost in the woods
- Secretly struggling with seasonal mood swings

Winter

- Drinking hot chocolate all day
- Watching all their favorite childhood movies

What's Your Secret?

If you had one thing that makes you so *you*, what would it be? We asked the signs to spill their secrets and here's what they had to say. Well, everyone but Scorpio, but we wouldn't expect anything less, to be honest.

What's my secret, you ask?

Check your Sun and Moon signs.

I'm an **ARIES** who can actively ignore reality in favor of my own perceptions.

I'm a **TAURUS** who can play the role of "down-to-earth" even when I'm stressed beyond belief.

I'm a **GEMINI** who can switch up my mood and my decisions at the drop of a hat.

I'm a **CANCER** who gets even moodier when people call me moody.

I'm a **LEO** who will need regular proof of how much you love me.

I'm a **VIRGO** who can picture literally every bad outcome of any situation.

I'm a **LIBRA** who can and will charm you into believing anything.

I'm a **SCORPIO** and I'll tell you mine if you tell me yours.

I'm a **SAGITTARIUS** who refuses to stay in a boring situation.

I'm a **CAPRICORN** who actually feels *a lot*, even when I don't share it.

I'm an **AQUARIUS** with a creative solution to any problem.

I'm a **PISCES** who will *escape* to my dreamworld when reality sucks.

Zodiac Takeout

Oh, takeout! Let me count the ways I love you . . . and what makes you like a zodiac sign! These aren't supposed to tell you what kind of food you should order. No, as weird and out-there as it might sound, some kinds of takeout have a *vibe*. Getting pizza is just a totally different experience than getting a fancy sushi boat. So think abstractly. We matched groups of two astrology signs' shared energy with some popular takeout types. *Bon appétit!*

Check your Sun, Moon, and Rising signs.

Aries and Sagittarius

Pizza

- They prefer things fast and exciting.
- "I'll try anything once" attitude . . . bring on the kimchi pizza!
- Up for late-night fun. Call at midnight and they're still open for business.
- Always a crowd favorite, because they're all so lovable.

Taurus and Capricorn

BBQ

- Taste like this? Maybe a bit pricey, but always totally worth it.
- Refuses to settle for boring; a variety of exciting sides is a must.
- Consistently top quality. Always genuine and reliable.
- Patience is key, both for awesome BBQ and these earth signs.

Gemini and Leo

Tacos

- Perfect at parties. Gemini, Leo, and tacos are all fun and full of character.
- Can be super spicy, when they're feeling like it.
- Aesthetically pleasing. The full package!
- Extra fun when paired with tequila.

Cancer and Virgo

Sushi

- Believes in quality over quantity.
- Perfectly precise. There's a subtle art to sushi, and to these signs!
- Truly distinctive and innovative, inside and out.
- Extra healthy. It's all about nourishing and flourishing.

Libra and Scorpio

Indian

- Spicy and exciting! Always brings a hot take to the table.
- Truly amazing, diverse tastes.
- Knows the importance of a beautiful presentation.
- Saucy as heck and lovin' it!

Aquarius and Pisces

Chinese

- Always there when you need 'em, 365 days a year!
- Great in a group setting. Takes all needs into consideration.
- An amazing companion for an all-night TV binge.
- Perfect amount of salty.

Halloween Costumes

Getting all dolled up—or maybe even all faux bloodied up—is the best part of Halloween! With the jack-o'-lanterns grinning and the kids calling "Trick or Treat," the signs are busy getting ready for a Halloween party. Each pair of signs share some similarities that make a costume just totally right for them. What's the perfect classic Halloween costume for you, based on your astrology sign? You can even make a combo costume out of your signs. Bring on the vampire starlet!

Check your Sun and Rising signs.

The Signs as Classic Costumes

OLD HOLLYWOOD STARLET

perfect pose in every photo

high luxury bitch

costume jewelry forever

talks in a accent all night

TAURUS + LEO

The Signs as Classic Costumes

VAMPIRE

contour perfectly on point

judging the costume contest

spooky but still pretty

sips red wine out of a fancy chalice

VIRGO + LIBRA

The **Signs** as **Classic Costumes**

HIPPIE

brings "special" brownies

already hippies at heart

all flower powered up!

kind hearted and creative

AQUARIUS + PISCES

What's Your Vampire Vibe?

When the Moon is out and the bats are flying, what's your vampy vibe? Are you more of a romantic sweetheart or a leather-clad cutie? We've compiled your vampire vibes based on your elemental type.

Check your Sun and Rising signs.

Fire
Aries, Leo, Sagittarius

- Castle-dwelling drama queens
- Starts a punk motorcycle gang
- Feeds on other vamps' drama
- Bored of living forever

Earth
Taurus, Virgo, Capricorn

- Terrifying when mad
- Thriving on four hundred years of acquired luxury
- Passing judgment on other vamps' dram
- Sparkly aesthetic on point

Air
Gemini, Libra, Aquarius

- Nocturnal party animals
- Leather and latex vibes
- Sits back and watches other vamps' drama
- Hostess with the most-ess

Water
Cancer, Scorpio, Pisces

- Low-key loves coffin naps
- Lacy Victorian dram looks
- Swept into the drama and hates it
- Getting flirty with the demons

What Mermaid Are You?

What kind of mermaid are you? Do you go full-on Disney babe mode? Or do you lean more toward the siren-style cutie? Each pair of signs here share some similarities, making them just the perfect blend of mythological sea babe!

Check your Sun and Rising signs.

Aries and Capricorn

- Starts a major coffee chain with a mermaid logo
- Refuses any offer of help
- Major boss babe attitude
- Swims their own way

Taurus and Libra

- Lives the full Aphrodite aesthetic
- Too busy enjoying life to respond to texts
- Swims away from even a ripple of conflict
- Flirts with sailors for fun

Gemini and Sagittarius

- Wishing for legs to explore more
- Will up and leave any boring situation
- True IDGAF attitude
- Makes waves with their opinions

Leo and Virgo

- Ultra-generous and might even grant a wish
- Running the entire underwater kingdom
- Disney-style mermaid: kind, great hair, and 100 percent genuine
- A bit bossy, but gets stuff done

Scorpio and Cancer

- Bewitching siren vibes
- Maintains an air of mystery
- Secretly loves a forbidden romance
- Loves to tempt the cryptid hunters

Aquarius and Pisces

- Organizes efforts to clean up the seas
- Overthinks at night, oversleeps in the morning
- Friends with all the creatures in the sea
- Siren song is on point

The Signs as Fairies

Do you believe in fairies? Do you step gingerly when you come across a ring of mushrooms in the woods, careful not to offend the fae? There's a whole world of fairy lore out there, and they can be as different from each other as humans. We tapped into some of the stories to find fairy-like traits for the signs, grouped by modality.

Check your Sun and Rising signs.

Cardinal

Aries, Cancer, Libra, Capricorn

- Thrives when jumping into something new
- Usually thinking more than they let on
- Can be pretty defensive when provoked
- Literally no patience for time-wasters

Fixed

Taurus, Leo, Scorpio, Aquarius

- Refuses to tolerate rude or impolite people
- Always down for a good gift or offering
- Trust them to always honor their promises
- Prefers living life on their own schedule

Mutable

Gemini, Virgo, Sagittarius, Pisces

- Have an undeniable magnetism to them
- Loves pulling off a good, harmless prank
- Known to talk with animals
- Seemingly born with chill vibes

Your Astrological Bouquet

Before you go, we've got a little something for you, darling. We picked you your very own astrological bouquet! There's a lot of meaning behind these beautiful buds. Practically every flower has symbolism associated with it in the language of flowers. These were all chosen to highlight some of the most beautiful qualities of the signs.

Check your Sun, Moon, and Rising signs.

Aries

Coreopsis, amaryllis, baby's breath

Sunny · resilient · sincere

Taurus

Carnation, eucalyptus, ranunculus

Entrancing · strong · charming

Gemini

Hibiscus, sage, lilac

Enthralling · keen · energetic

Cancer

Camellia, blue violet, forget-me-not

Wistful · intuitive · unforgettable

Leo

Tiger lily, crocus, statice
Proud · original · impressive

Virgo

Magnolia, chrysanthemum, iris
Dignified · remarkable · bright

Libra

Peony, hypericum berry, daisy
Radiant · effervescent · fascinating

Scorpio

Fern, heliotrope, zinnia
Mystical · devoted · determined

Sagittarius

Edelweiss, jasmine, sunflower

Audacious · friendly · optimistic

Capricorn

Dahlia, angelica, clematis

Elegant · ingenious · resourceful

Aquarius

Aster, globe amaranth, black-eyed Susan

Perceptive · open-minded · genuine

Pisces

Calla lily, goldenrod, hyacinth

Tender · inspiring · playful

Last Stop!

Well, this is the last stop on this train, cosmic hottie. And man oh man, we want to thank you so much for taking the ride with us. Hopefully, you're a little more confident in your understanding of your Sun, Moon, and Rising signs. We hope this journey was informative, magical, and, above all, *fun!*

What's next on your astrological travels, you might be wondering? If you've been having a blast learning about the zodiac and feeling out all the ways it influences your life and relationships, then we encourage you to stay curious! After all, we really only focused on your Big Three placements. Your Sun, Moon, and Rising signs, while for sure the most prominent placements in your life are just the starting point. There's a whole chart full of planets for you to explore! Every single one of your placements has a part to play in your life. That's not even dipping a toe into the astrological houses, aspects between your planets, or how transits might affect your life.

Astrology is a wild, expansive topic and no matter where you are on your path, you can always learn something new. Don't put pressure on yourself to understand everything instantly. Just like any other field of study, it takes time to really absorb the information and see how it manifests in your life. Anyone can read about something; it's when you live it that you truly *understand* it. Look at us—we've been studying astrology for more than a decade and still have those sudden moments of clarity, when something in our charts *finally* snaps into focus.

Plus, it's pretty cool when you can reliably guess someone's sign correctly!

It's super satisfying when you're able to recognize the forces that are influencing your life. Hopefully, you're now on a path that allows you to see those connections, to bring an area of struggle in your life into sudden focus. You have to see the obstacles in your way before you can overcome them. Astrology is a very powerful tool of self-reflection, but it's also there when you need something to lighten your mood. Life doesn't need to be all significant revelations and trials! Sometimes, you just want to laugh at Sagittarius's sometimes-endearing, sometimes-frustrating tendency to have no filter whatsoever, or Virgo saying "you're" in the group chat. And that's okay.

Can we ask one more thing? If you haven't done so already, check us out on social media. You'll find us as The Pulp Girls on all the things. We always strive to create an inclusive, interactive space, and you can bet you'll find a lot more astrology fun from us there in the future. Thank you again for being here, and for being your beautiful, breathtaking, cosmic self!

Mini Glossary

The Signs

Glyph	Sign	Symbol
♈	Aries	The Ram
♉	Taurus	The Bull
♊	Gemini	The Twins
♋	Cancer	The Crab
♌	Leo	The Lion
♍	Virgo	The Maiden
♎	Libra	The Scales
♏	Scorpio	The Scorpion
♐	Sagittarius	The Archer
♑	Capricorn	The Sea Goat
♒	Aquarius	The Water Bearer
♓	Pisces	The Fish

The Planets and Ascendant

Glyph	Placement	Influences
☉	Sun	Identity and Ego
☽	Moon	Emotions and Needs
ASC	Ascendant	Interactions and Appearance
☿	Mercury	Communication and Reason
♂	Mars	Action and Passion
♀	Venus	Love and Beauty
♃	Jupiter	Luck and Abundance
♄	Saturn	Discipline and Responsibility
♅	Uranus	Individuality and Rebellion
♆	Neptune	Dreams and Intuition
♇	Pluto	Transformation and Rebirth

Thank You!

Sending a beautiful, heartfelt thank you to everyone who made this book possible. To everyone at Quarto who helped us along the way, thank you from the bottom of our hearts, especially, Rage for believing in us and our vision. A big thank you to our editor, Keyla, who brought it all together and helped to make this dream a reality.

Thank you to our mom Claire, who always believed in us! 💜 Thank you for being there for us as we navigate our unconventional life path.

Another thank you goes out to Dan for always being there to make the atmosphere as perfect as possible for creative flow!

We also want to send each and every one of our supporters and followers our endless thanks for being there and making this possible.
Love you all, you cosmic hotties!

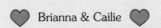 Brianna & Cailie

About the Authors

Cailie and Brianna are the co-founders of The Pulp Girls. They are two sisters making magic with vintage art and astrology. Cailie is The Pulp Girls' resident illustrator. You'll find her gorgeous artwork all over this book! She draws artistic inspiration from all sorts of different outlets: vintage fashion illustration, advertising, graphics, fairy tales, art zines . . . you name it! Plus, she's a Taurus Sun, Capricorn Moon, and Libra Rising. In case you're new to astrology, those are some strong Venus vibes, meaning she's got quite the aesthetic sense! Brianna has always had a way with words, pairing expression and creation with a captivating voice. She's an Aries Sun, Pisces Moon, and Leo Rising. She's always found inspiration in fantasy worlds and the occult. Such a Pisces Moon!

Find them online:

@thepulpgirls 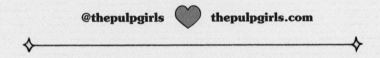 thepulpgirls.com

Also available from Quarto and the Pulp Girls